Ninja Dual Zone Air Fryer Cookbook UK 2023

1001 Days Affordable and Crispy Recipes for Your
Whole Family to Master Your Ninja
Dual Zone Air Fryer

Nancy R. Lara

Disclaimer Notice:

Please note the information contained within this document is for educational and entertainment purposes only. All effort has been executed to present accurate, up to date, reliable, complete information. No warranties of any kind are declared or implied. Readers acknowledge that the author is not engaged in the rendering of legal, financial, medical or professional advice. The content within this book has been derived from various sources. Please consult a licensed professional before attempting any techniques outlined in this book.

By reading this document, the reader agrees that under no circumstances is the author responsible for any losses, direct or indirect, that are incurred as a result of the use of the information contained within this document, including, but not limited to, errors, omissions, or inaccuracies.

Contents

Introduction

The Ninja DualZone Airfryer Cookbook: The Beginner's Guide To Cooking With This Unique Cookware

If you've recently purchased a Ninja Dual Zone Air Fryer, then you're probably wondering what to do with it. Luckily for you, we have the perfect guide: A Ninja Dual Zone Air Fryer Cookbook for Beginners! This cookbook is the perfect place to start if you're looking to master your new air fryer. We'll show you how to use the appliance to its fullest potential, as well as teach you some of our favourite recipes and techniques. So get ready to explore the wonderful world of air frying with us!

Surprising Fact; I didn't always love to cook!

I was never one of those kids who loved to help out in the kitchen. I would much rather have been outside playing with my friends than stuck inside cooking. It wasn't until I moved out of my parents' house and had to start cooking for myself that I began to appreciate all the hard work that goes into making a meal.

Now, I love to cook! I find it therapeutic and relaxing, and I love experimenting with new recipes. The Ninja Dual Zone Air Fryer is the perfect tool for someone like me who loves to

cook. It's so versatile and easy to use, and it produces perfectly cooked food every time.

If you're someone who doesn't love to cook, I urge you to give it a try. You might just surprise yourself!

I always found worst thing about cooking is having to use the right cooking methods and doing them correctly. This can be a real challenge for beginners, and remains true even when it comes to air frying. However, with the Ninja Dual Zone Air Fryer Cookbook for Beginners, you'll have everything you need to master air frying in no time. This cookbook includes detailed instructions on how to use your air fryer, as well as recipes for a variety of delicious dishes. Whether you're looking for a quick and easy weeknight meal or something more elaborate for a special occasion, you'll find it in this cookbook. With the Ninja Dual Zone Air Fryer Cookbook for Beginners, you'll be an air frying pro in no time!

How the airfryer changed my approach to cooking!

When I first started cooking, I would always shy away from recipes that called for deep frying. It just seemed like too much of a hassle— having to heat up all that oil, and then dealing with the mess afterwards. But then I got an air fryer, and it completely changed my approach to cooking.

Now, I can easily make all sorts of recipes that call for deep frying, without any of the hassle. The air fryer does all the work for me, and cleanup is a breeze. Plus, it's healthier than traditional deep frying, so I feel good about what I'm eating.

If you're thinking about getting an air fryer,

or if you already have one and are wondering what to do with it, check out this cookbook. It's packed with delicious recipes that are easy to make, and sure to please everyone at the table.

What type of foods can the airfryer cook well (and what foods to avoid!)

When it comes to air fryers, there are a few things to keep in mind. First, they work best with small, quick-cooking items. T
his means that foods like chicken wings, french fries, and mozzarella sticks are all great candidates for air frying. However, there are certain foods that don't fare so well in an air fryer. These include large cuts of meat, whole chickens, and anything that requires a long cooking time.

So what type of foods can the air fryer cook well? Here are a few examples:

-*Chicken wings*
-*French fries*
-*Mozzarella sticks*
-*Vegetables like broccoli and cauliflower*
-*Fish fillets*
-*Potatoes (baked or roasted)*

And here are a few examples of foods to avoid:
-*Whole chickens or turkeys*
-*Large cuts of meat like steaks or ribs*
-*Anything that requires a long cooking time like casseroles*

Introduction to the Ninja Dual Zone Air Fryer

In Ninja's Dual Zone Air Fryer, there are two ways to cook your food. The first is the traditional air fryer method, which uses hot air to cook food quickly and evenly. The second is the Ninja method, which uses infrared heat to cook food from the inside out.

With the Ninja Dual Zone Air Fryer, you can cook multiple types of food at the same time without flavour transfer. This means that you can cook chicken and fish at the same time without worrying about the fish tasting like chicken.

The Ninja Dual Zone Air Fryer also has a dehydrator function, which means that you can make your own dried fruit or beef jerky.

The Ninja Dual Zone Air Fryer is a unique appliance that has two independent cooking zones that can be used simultaneously. This means that you can cook two different foods at the same time, or cook one large dish.

The Ninja Dual Zone Air Fryer also has a built in Rapid Air Circulation System that circulates hot air around food for even cooking. This ensures that your food is cooked evenly, and prevents it from sticking to the basket. In addition, the Ninja Dual Zone Air Fryer comes with a variety of accessories, including a multi-purpose rack, which is perfect for cooking multiple items at once.

It also has a removable drip tray that makes cleanup quick and easy. Finally, the Ninja Dual Zone Air Fryer has a sleek design that will look great on your countertop. It's also compact and lightweight, making it easy to store away when not in use.

Basic Cooking Techniques Using the Ninja Dual Zone Air Fryer

One of the great things about the Ninja Dual Zone Air Fryer is that it can do so much more than just air fry food. It can also be used for basic cooking techniques like baking, roasting, and even dehydrating food.

In this section we will go over some of the basic cooking techniques you can use with your air fryer to make delicious meals.

Air Frying:

Air frying is a healthier alternative to deep frying as it uses less oil and circulates hot air around the food to cook it evenly. To air fry with your Ninja Dual Zone Air Fryer, simply place your food in the basket, select the air fry function, and set the temperature. The air fryer will do the rest!

Baking:

The Ninja Dual Zone Air Fryer can also be used for baking. Simply preheat the oven by selecting the bake function and setting the temperature. Then place your food on the baking rack and cook according to your recipe.

Roasting:

Roasting is a great way to cook meat or vegetables and bring out their natural flavors. To roast with your Ninja Dual Zone Air Fryer, simply place your food in the basket, select the roast function, and set the temperature. The air fryer will do the rest!

Dehydrating:

The Ninja Dual Zone Airfryer is the perfect kitchen appliance for dehydrating foods. With two independent cooking zones, you can dehydrate foods in the top zone while air frying foods in the bottom zone. The top zone features a dehydrate function that circulates hot air over the food, causing it to lose moisture and become dried out. The bottom zone features an air fry function that circulates hot air around the food, resulting in a crispy, fried finish.To dehydrate foods in the Ninja Dual Zone Airfryer, simply place the food in the top cooking zone and select the dehydrate function. Set the desired temperature and time, and the Airfryer will do the rest. Once the food is dried out, it can be stored in an airtight container for future use.

How does the Airfryer cook food?

The Ninja Dual Zone Air Fryer is a unique appliance that allows you to cook food in a healthier way. The secret is in the technology. Here's the science to how an airfryer works!

- Air fryers work by circulating hot air around food. This method of cooking is similar to convection cooking, which is often used in professional kitchens.
- The difference is that air fryers use less oil, which makes them a healthier option for home cooks. When food is cooked in an air fryer, it is exposed to high heat. This causes the surface of the food to cook quickly, while the inside remains moist.
- This results in food that is crispy on the outside and tender on the inside.
- One of the benefits of using an air fryer is that it can help you save calories. Studies have shown that food cooked in an air fryer requires up to 75% less oil than food cooked in a traditional deep fryer. This means that you can enjoy your favourite fried foods without all of the unhealthy fats.
- Another benefit of air frying is that it can help you reduce your carbon footprint. Air fryers use less energy than traditional ovens, so they are more environmentally friendly. In addition, they do not produce any harmful emissions, making them a safe choice for your home.

How to clean and maintain the Ninja Dual Zone Air Fryer

One of the great things about the Ninja Dual Zone Air Fryer is that it is very easy to clean

and maintain. Here are a few simple tips to keep your air fryer in tip-top shape:

- Never use abrasive cleaners or scrubbers on the air fryer basket or cooking pot, as this can damage the nonstick coating. Instead, simply wipe them down with a damp cloth after each use.
- The oil drip tray can be removed for easy cleaning. Simply wash it in warm, soapy water and dry thoroughly before replacing.
- If you notice any build-up of grease or food residue on the air fryer's heating elements, simply wipe them down with a damp cloth.
- Always unplug the air fryer and allow it to cool completely before cleaning.

Tips and Tricks for Using the Ninja Dual Zone Air Fryer

The Ninja Dual Zone Air Fryer is a versatile kitchen appliance that can be used for a variety of cooking tasks. Here are some tips and tricks for using the Ninja Dual Zone Air Fryer:

- 1. Use the preheat function to cook food more evenly.
- 2. Place food in the basket with the larger side down so that it cooks more evenly.
- 3. Use the dual-zone feature to cook two different types of food at the same time.
- 4. Use the pause function to stop cooking if needed.
- 5. Use the keep warm function to keep food warm until ready to serve.

Why you need the Ninja Dual Zone Airfryer!

The Ninja Dual Zone Air Fryer is a versatile kitchen appliance that can help you cook a variety of foods. If you're looking for an air fryer that can handle both small and large quantities of food, the Ninja Dual Zone Air

Fryer is a great option.

Here are some of the reasons why you need the Ninja Dual Zone Air Fryer:

1. It can cook large quantities of food.
The Ninja Dual Zone Air Fryer has two cooking zones, so it can accommodate a lot of food. This is perfect if you're cooking for a crowd or if you want to make enough food for leftovers.

2. It's versatile.
The Ninja Dual Zone Air Fryer can be used to cook a variety of foods, from chicken wings to French fries. You can also use it to bake, so it's perfect for those who like to experiment with their cooking.

3. It's easy to use.
The Ninja Dual Zone Air Fryer is very easy to use, even for beginners. The controls are straightforward and the appliance comes with an instruction manual that will guide you through the cooking process step-by-step.

4. It's affordable.
The Ninja Dual Zone Air Fryer is very affordable, especially when compared to other air fryers on the market. If you're looking for a quality air fryer without breaking the bank, the Ninja Dual Zone Air Fryer is a great

Possible Risks to avoid when using the airfryer!

When using an air fryer, there are a few possible risks to avoid in order to ensure a safe and successful cooking experience. Here are a few tips:

- Be sure to read the manual carefully before use. This will help you understand the proper way to operate your air fryer and avoid any potential risks.
- Never leave the air fryer unattended while in use. This could lead to serious accidents or fires.
- Be careful when handling hot food or oil. Use oven mitts or gloves to avoid burns.
- Make sure the air fryer is properly

ventilated. Some models require ventilation holes to be uncovered during use, so be sure to check the manual for specific instructions.

By following these simple tips, you can help avoid any potential risks when using an air fryer and enjoy delicious, healthy meals with peace of mind!

Q&A

Q: What is an air fryer?

A: An air fryer is a kitchen appliance that uses hot air to cook food. It typically has a basket or drawer that holds the food to be cooked, and a fan that circulates the hot air around the food.

Q: How does an air fryer work?

A: Air fryers work by circulating hot air around the food in their baskets or drawers. This hot air cooks the food, and the circulating motion helps to ensure even cooking.

Q: What can you cook in an air fryer?

A: You can cook almost anything in an air fryer! Many people use them to cook chicken, fish, or vegetables, but you can also use them to cook French fries, onion rings, and even desserts!

Q: Do I need any special equipment to use an air fryer?

A: No, you don't need any special equipment to use an air fryer. All you need is the air fryer itself and something to put the food in (like a basket or drawer). Some models come with accessories like tongs or racks, but they're not necessary.

Q: What are some of the benefits of using an air fryer?

A: There are many benefits of using an air fryer! One of the top benefits is that they're very versatile – you can cook almost anything in them.

Q: What types of food can I cook in an air fryer?

A: You can cook almost anything in an air fryer! However, some foods work better than others. Foods that are typically fried, such as chicken or french fries, come out especially well in an air fryer.

Q: Do I need to preheat my Ninja Dual Zone Air Fryer before cooking?

A: Yes, you should preheat your air fryer before cooking. This will help ensure that your food cooks evenly.

Q: Are there any downsides to using an air fryer?

A: One downside of air fryers is that they can be more expensive than other kitchen appliances. Additionally, some people find that air-fried foods can be less crispy than those fried in oil.

Q: What are some of the features of the Ninja Dual Zone Air Fryer?

A: Some of the features of the Ninja Dual Zone Air Fryer include an advanced airflow system, a ceramic-coated cooking basket, and a detachable dishwasher-safe drip tray. It also has a digital display with pre-set cooking functions, so you can easily choose the perfect settings for your food.

Q: How do I clean the Ninja Dual Zone Air Fryer?

A: The Ninja Dual Zone Air Fryer is easy to clean thanks to its detachable dishwasher-safe drip tray. Simply remove the tray and wash it in your dishwasher.

Granola in an Air Fryer

Preparation time: 15 minutes
Cooking time: 35 minutes
Serves: 12 servings

Ingredients:

- 227g Maple syrup
- 115 ml olive oil
- 260g rolled oats
- 40g sunflower seeds
- 1 1/2 teaspoons of ground cinnamon
- Optional milk and other toppings for serving
- 2 teaspoons of vanilla extract
- 1 large egg white
- 85g chopped almonds
- 40g almond flour

Method:

1. Preheat your air fryer to 170 degrees Celsius and line your air fryer tray with baking paper.
2. Combine maple syrup, vanilla, olive oil, egg white, and 1/2 teaspoon salt in a medium bowl. Oats, almonds, sunflower seeds, almond flour, and cinnamon are combined in a big basin. Mix well before adding the maple syrup mixture to the dry ingredients.
3. Evenly press the mixture onto the prepared air fryer tray using the back of spoon or wet hands.
4. Bake for 25 to 30 minutes, rotating the tray once halfway through and opening your air fryer twice to let steam out. There is no need to mix the granola.
5. Let cool and break into chunks when the granola reaches room temperature.

Air-Fried Bacon with Glaze

Preparation time: 2 minutes
Cooking time: 6 minutes
Serves: 2 people

Ingredients:

- 6 Rashers of Streaky bacon
- 1 tablespoon maple syrup
- Ketchup to serve
- 3 tablespoons of caster sugar
- 1 tablespoon butter

Method:

1. Set your air fryer to 200 degrees Celsius.
2. Arrange your bacon rashers in a single layer in the air fryer tray.
3. Melt your butter, sugar and syrup in a saucepan until the syrup and butter have dissolved

completely.

4. Cook for 5 minutes, turning at 3 minutes.
5. For the final minute, brush with the glaze on both sides and cook until the glaze is caramelised.
6. Serve with ketchup!

Air Fryer Spicy Eggs with Cheese and Chives

Preparation time: 1 minute
Cooking time: 5 minutes
Serves: 1 person

Ingredients:

- 2 Eggs
- 1/4 Teaspoon of Salt
- 1/4 Teaspoon of Black Pepper
- 1 teaspoon chives
- 25g grated cheddar cheese
- Tabasco sauce to serve

Method:

1. Line your air fryer tray with baking paper.
2. Crack two eggs into the air fryer being careful not to break the yolks.
3. Sprinkle with the salt and pepper.
4. Add your chives.
5. Cook for three to four minutes on 190 degrees Celsius.
6. For the final minute or two, add your grated cheese and take the eggs out of the fryer when the cheese has melted.
7. Serve with a generous drizzle of tabasco sauce!

Air Fryer Sausage Omelette

Preparation time: 2 minutes
Cooking time: 10 - 15 minutes
Serves: 6 people

Ingredients:

- 6 sausages of your choice, sliced
- 6 beaten eggs
- 2 small onions, finely chopped
- 20g button mushrooms, chopped
- 10g cherry tomatoes, chopped
- 10g red pepper, chopped

Method:

1. Combine all of the ingredients in a large bowl and mix.
2. Make sure the egg thoroughly covers all of the ingredients.
3. Line the air fryer tray with a layer of the mixture and cook on 190 degrees Celsius for 10-15 minutes.
4. Repeat the cooking instructions until all of the mixture is used up.

Easy Air Fryer Vegetarian Omelette

Preparation time: 8 minutes
Cooking time: 8 to 10 minutes
Serves: 1 person

Ingredients:

- 3 Eggs
- 1 small white onion
- 20 g grated cheddar cheese
- 1/4 teaspoon of black pepper
- 3 cherry tomatoes
- 1 teaspoon of olive oil
- 1/4 teaspoon of salt
- 3 small mushrooms

Method:

1. Preheat your air fryer at 180 degrees Celsius.
2. Whisk your eggs thoroughly together with your salt and pepper.
3. Finely chop your mushrooms, onions, tomatoes and ham.
4. Add the mushrooms, onions and tomatoes to your whisked eggs.
5. Use the olive oil to grease your air fryer tray.
6. Add the egg and other ingredients to your air fryer tray and cook for eight to ten minutes, adding the grated cheese halfway through.

Easy Breakfast Burritos

Preparation time: 10 minutes
Cooking time: 15 minutes
Serves: 2 people

Ingredients:

- 4 large flour tortillas
- 2 red peppers
- 2 large sausages
- 3 mushrooms
- 1/4 teaspoon of salt
- 3 large eggs
- 4 frozen hash browns
- 4 rashers of bacon
- 2 tomatoes
- 1/4 teaspoon of black pepper

Method:

1. First, cut all of your ingredients into small chunks. You want to be able to mix them enough

to have a bite containing all of the ingredients when you are eating your burrito.

2. Place your chopped ingredients into the tray and cook for 10 minutes at 190 degrees Celsius.

3. While those ingredients are cooking, crack your eggs, add salt and pepper and whisk thoroughly. When the other ingredients are finished cooking you can place the eggs into your air fryer and cook for around 3 minutes for scrambled eggs.

4. When your eggs are finished, combine all of your ingredients and place them into the tortillas. Wrap like a burrito and cook for about 3 minutes in your air fryer or until the outside of the burrito is a little crispy.

Easy Pancakes

Preparation time: 5 minutes
Cooking time: 20 minutes
Serves: 8 pancakes

Ingredients:

- 105 g plain white flour
- 240 ml whole milk
- 1/2 tablespoon of butter
- 1/4 teaspoon of salt
- 2 large eggs
- Syrup to serve

Method:

1. Salt and flour are sifted together in a bowl.
2. Whisk in the milk and eggs before adding them to the mixture. While not being excessively thin, the batter should flow. Leave alone for a while.
3. Heat your air fryer to 190 degrees Celsius and pour a thin layer of mixture into the cake or pizza pan attachment. Make sure the pan is well greased with cooking spray or melted butter.
4. Cook each individual pancake for around 4 minutes then turn and cook for a further 3. Repeat for each pancake.
5. Serve with a generous drizzle of syrup!

Easy Breakfast Muffins

Preparation time:15 minutes
Cooking time: 25 minutes
Serves: 4 people

Ingredients:

- 1 tablespoon of oil
- 1 red pepper, finely chopped
- 6 large eggs
- 1/4 teaspoon of smoked paprika
- 150g broccoli, finely chopped
- 2 spring onions, sliced
- 1 tablespoon of whole milk
- 50g cheddar

Method:

1. Heat your air fryer to 200 degrees Celsius and prepare silicon muffin cases with a thin layer

of oil or melted butter.

2. Lightly fry the broccoli, pepper and spring onions in your air fryer for 5 minutes.

3. Whisk your eggs, milk, smoked paprika and half of your cheese together.

4. Add your fried broccoli, peppers and spring onions to the mixture and add half of your cheese.

5. Pour your mixture into the muffin cases then sprinkle the remaining cheese on the top of the muffins.

6. Fry in the air fryer for around 17 minutes or until the cheese is melted and the muffins are golden brown.

Air Fryer Cheese Toasties

Preparation time: 5 minutes
Cooking time: 8 minutes
Serves: 2 people

Ingredients:

- 4 slices of soft white bread
- 4 slices of cheese (cheddar works best)
- 2 teaspoons of cream cheese
- 3 tablespoons of butter
- 2 slices of ham
- 1 teaspoon of chives

Method:

1. Coat all sides of your slices of bread with butter.

2. Lay two slices of bread into your air fryer basket.

3. Combine the chives with the cream cheese and spread thoroughly over the bread.

4. Place cheese slices on the top of the bread with the ham and cover with another slice of bread, completing the sandwiches.

5. Fry in your air fryer at 180 degrees Celsius for 4 minutes then flip and cook for another 4 minutes or until the cheese has melted and the bread is golden brown.

Chocolate Brownie Oats

Preparation time: 10 minutes
Cooking time: 10 minutes
Serves: 2 people

Ingredients:

- 1/2 large banana
- 1 teaspoon of vanilla extract
- 1 tablespoon of coco powder
- 1/2 teaspoon of baking powder
- 1 tablespoon of golden syrup
- 1 large egg
- 60 ml whole milk
- 100g rolled oats

Method:

1. Lightly grease your air fryer tray.

2. Pour all of your ingredients into a blender and blend until super smooth.

3. Pour the mixture into your air fryer tray.

4. Air fry for 10 minutes at 160 degrees Celsius.

Blueberry Muffin Baked Oats

Preparation time: 10 minutes
Cooking time: 10 minutes
Serves: 2 people

Ingredients:

- 1 large banana
- 1 teaspoon of vanilla extract
- large handful of blueberries
- 1/2 teaspoon of baking powder
- 1 tablespoon of golden syrup
- 1 large egg
- 60 ml whole milk
- 100g rolled oats

Method:

1. Lightly grease your air fryer tray.

2. Pour all of your ingredients into a blender and blend until super smooth.

3. Gently mix in your blueberries being careful not to crush any.

4. Pour the mixture into your air fryer tray.

5. Air fry for 10 minutes at 160 degrees Celsius.

Breakfast Lasagna

Preparation time: 15 minutes
Cooking time: 25 minutes
Serves: 4 people

Ingredients:

- 8 rasher of bacon
- 4 large tortillas
- 1 large handful of cheese
- 1 red pepper (diced)
- 3 mushrooms (diced)
- 4 sausages
- 4 large eggs
- 1 small white onion (diced)
- 1 tomato (diced)
- 3 hashbrowns

Method:

1. Cook your bacon, sausages, tomatoes, onion, mushrooms, pepper and hash browns in the air fryer in groups so nothing overlaps. Cook at 200 degrees Celsius for about 6 minutes per group.

2. Next, scramble your eggs and place in the air fryer basket for 3 minutes or until cooked fully.

3. Layer one tortilla then some sausage, then bacon, then tomatoes, mushrooms, onions, pepper and hash browns and top with some eggs and cheese.

4. On top of this place another tortilla and repeat until all the ingredients are used.

5. Air fry for a further 5 minutes until the cheese has melted and the tortillas are golden brown.

Breakfast Pizza

Preparation time: 15 minutes
Cooking time: 20 minutes
Serves: 1 person

Ingredients:

- 50 g grated cheese
- 2 tablespoons of tomato puree
- 1 tomato (chopped)
- 1 chopped sausage
- 1 large tortilla
- 1 mushroom (chopped)
- 25 g baked beans
- 2 rashers of bacon (chopped)

Method:

1. Start by frying your sausage and bacon in the air fryer for 6 minutes at 200 degrees Celsius.
2. Spread the tomato puree over the tortilla.
3. Cover the tortilla with the other ingredients trying not to overlap too many in the same places.
4. Finish with the cheese over the top of the pizza. Then add your sausage and bacon.
5. Air fry for 10 minutes or until the tortilla is golden brown and the cheese is fully melted.

Honey Porridge

Preparation time: 5 minutes
Cooking time: 10 minutes
Serves: 2 people

Ingredients:

- 1 large banana
- 1 teaspoon of vanilla extract
- 1/2 teaspoon of cinnamon
- 60 ml whole milk
- 100g rolled oats
- 1 tablespoon of golden syrup
- 1 large egg
- 3 tablespoons of honey
- 1/2 teaspoon of baking powder
- 1/2 teaspoon of ground ginger

Method:

1. Combine all of the dry ingredients.
2. Mash the banana separately.
3. Whisk the egg and add to the banana.
4. Add the banana, egg, milk, golden syrup and honey to the dry ingredients.
5. Mix thoroughly. Add more milk if the mixture is too dry.
6. Spread across air fryer basket and fry at 160 degrees Celsius for 10 minutes.

Quick Air-Fryer Fish and Chips

Preparation time: 15 minutes
Cooking time: 25 minutes
Serves: 4 people

Ingredients:

For the Chips:
- 2 Tablespoons of Olive Oil
- 1/4 Teaspoon of Pepper
- 1/4 Teaspoon of Salt
- 450g Potatoes

For the Fish:
- 1 Large Egg
- 1/4 Teaspoon of Pepper
- 450 g Fillets of Cod or Haddock
- 80g Crushed Cornflakes
- 2 Tablespoons of Water
- 1/4 Teaspoon of Salt
- 42 g All-Purpose Flour

Method:

1. Preheat your air fryer to 200 degrees Celsius and start peeling your potatoes. Then you can cut the potatoes into chunky chip-sized pieces.
2. Grab a large mixing bowl and combine the oil, salt and pepper then toss your chopped potatoes in the mixture.
3. Next, place your potatoes in single-layer batches in your air fryer and cook for five to eight minutes. Remove your potatoes, turn them and place them back into the air fryer for a further five to ten minutes until crispy.
4. Whilst your chips are cooking, mix the flour, salt and pepper in a bowl.
5. Then whisk your large egg with the water in a separate bowl and in another bowl prepare your crushed cornflakes.
6. Take the fish fillets and dip them in the flour then the egg then the cornflakes.
7. Once your chips have finished you can place your fish in the air fryer tray and cook for around ten minutes, turning at the halfway point. Warm your chips in the basket and serve them together with the fish once hot!

Crispy Potato Salad

Preparation time: 10 minutes
Cooking time: 25 minutes
Serves: 4 people

Ingredients:
- 2 tablespoons olive oil
- 185g mayonnaise

- 40 g french onion soup mix
- 4 rashers bacon
- 1 tablespoon lemon juice
- 1 kg baby potatoes, halved
- 125 g sour cream
- 1/2 bunch chopped chives

Method:

1. Mix together the oil, 60 g mayonnaise and the soup mix.
3. Add the potato and combine.
3. Place into air fryer basket and fry for 15 minutes at 200 degrees Celsius.
4. Add the bacon and fry at 160 degrees Celsius for a further 10 minutes.
5. Mix together the remaining mayonnaise, sour cream, lemon juice and chives. Pour over the potatoes and serve.

Accordion Potatoes with Onion

Preparation time: 20 minutes

Cooking time: 20 minutes

Serves: 4 people

Ingredients:

- 4 large potatoes peeled
- 40 g french onion soup mix
- 150 g softened cream cheese
- 4 chopped green shallots
- 50 g vegetable oil
- 150 g sour cream
- 150g egg mayonnaise

Method:

1. Cut potatoes length ways into 1 cm thick pieces.
2. Partially cut the strips to make the accordion shape.
3. Pat potatoes dry.
4. Place skewer through the potatoes and fan out the accordion shape.
5. Mix the oil and 1 tablespoon of the soup mix.
6. Brush over the potatoes.
7. Cook at 180 degrees Celsius for 15 minutes.
8. Mix the cheese, sour cream, mayonnaises and soup mix in a bowl. Then add the shallots and mix again.
9. Serve the potatoes with the dip.

Air Fried Ice Cream

Preparation time: 12 hours

Cooking time: 15 minutes

Serves: 12 people

Ingredients:

- 450 g ice cream
- 3 eggs
- 300g crushed digestive biscuits
- 1 1/2 tablespoons milk

Method:

1. Freeze a baking tray.
2. Scoop ice cream into 12 balls and place on tray.
3. Freeze overnight.
4. Put the crushed biscuits in a bowl and roll the ice cream in the biscuits.
5. Freeze for another hour.
6. Whisk together the eggs and milk and roll ice cream balls in the mixture then more biscuits.
7. Freeze for another hour.
8. Preheat air fryer at 200 degrees Celsius.
9. Fry ice cream balls for 2 minutes each. Serve immediately.

Bread Roll Dip

Preparation time: 35 minutes
Cooking time: 30 minutes
Serves: 6 people

Ingredients:

- 450 g crusty bread rolls
- 1 tablespoon olive oil
- 3 crushed garlic cloves
- 200 g sour cream
- 75g shredded cheddar
- 3 thinly sliced shallots
- 250 g frozen spinach, thawed out
- 1 chopped onion
- 250 g cream cheese
- 125ml cream
- 35 g french onion soup mix

Method:

1. Cut off the tops of the bread rolls.
2. Scoop out the inner part of the bread.
3. Place all the bread into air fryer and fry for 8 minutes at 160 degrees Celsius.
4. Fry in a frying pan the onion and garlic for 5 minutes.
5. Next, add the spinach, cream cheese, sour cream, cream, cheese and soup mix. Stir until mixed.
6. Stir in the shallots and remove from heat.
7. Fill the rolls with the mixture.
8. Cover with foil and fry in air fryer for 15 minutes at 160 degrees Celsius. Remove foil and fry for a final 5 minutes.

Quiche Lorraine

Preparation time: 20 minutes
Cooking time: 40 minutes
Serves: 4 people

Ingredients:

- 1 thawed sheet of frozen puff pastry
- 175 g rindless bacon cut into batons
- 5 eggs
- 125ml milk
- 2 teaspoons olive oil
- 1 chopped brown onion
- 125 ml thickened cream
- 100 g grated cheese

Method:

1. Line air fryer cake or pizza pan with the pastry.
2. Air fry for 6 minutes at 180 degrees Celsius,
3. Fry bacon in a frying pan for 5 minutes then fry the onion with the bacon for a further 5 minutes.
4. Whisk the eggs, cream and milk in a medium bowl.
5. Add the bacon mixture to the base then pour over the egg mixture.
6. Top with the grated cheese.
7. Cook at 160 degrees Celsius for 30 minutes.

Potato Kiev

Preparation time: 30 minutes
Cooking time: 50 minutes
Serves: 4 people

Ingredients:

- 1 kg white potatoes
- 4 crushed garlic cloves
- 100 g grated cheddar
- 2 beaten eggs
- 100g breadcrumbs
- 100g chopped butter
- 1 tablespoon chopped chives
- 40 g white flour
- 2 tablespoons milk

Method:

1. Air fry potatoes for 30 minutes at 180 degrees Celsius.
2. Let cool then mash.
3. Combine the butter, chives, garlic and any other seasonings.
4. Shape butter into a log on baking paper then place in the fridge until solid.
5. Mix potatoes with cheese.
6. Put the flour in one bowl and the eggs and milk into another. In a third bowl place the breadcrumbs.
7. Roll potato into balls with the butter mix in the middle.
8. Coat the balls in flour then egg then breadcrumbs and place in the air fryer basket.
9. Air fry at 180 degrees Celsius for 10 minutes. Fry in batches or two or three.

French Toast Strips

Preparation time: 20 minutes
Cooking time: 1 hour
Serves: 6 people

Ingredients:

- 1 loaf of almost stale white bread
- 250ml milk
- 1 teaspoon ground cinnamon
- 60g melted butter
- 8 eggs
- 1 tablespoon caster sugar
- 1 teaspoon vanilla extract

Method:

1. Cut bread into 3 cm strips.
2. Whisk eggs, milk, sugar, cinnamon and vanilla.
3. Line air fryer tray with baking paper.
4. Soak bread in the egg mixture for 1 minute each.
5. Shake off excess mixture and place the bread in air fryer tray.
6. Cook at 180 degrees Celsius for 3 minutes then brush with melted butter and cook for another 3 minutes.
7. Repeat until all the bread is used.

Feta Filo Parcels

Preparation time: 20 minutes
Cooking time: 15 minutes
Serves: 24 parcels

Ingredients:

- 200g feta
- 2 tablespoons grated lemon rind
- 2 teaspoons black sesame seeds
- 12 sheets filo pastry
- 2 tablespoons shredded mint

Method:

1. Preheat air fryer to 180 degrees Celsius.
2. Line air fryer tray with baking paper.
3. Cut feta into 1 cm cubes.
4. Spray sheets of filo with cooking spray.
5. Lay pieces of feta in the centre of the pastry and sprinkle with lemon and mint.
6. Form 24 parcels filled with feta.
7. Sprinkle with sesame seeds and air fry for 12-15 minutes.

Pavlova

Preparation time: 40 minutes
Cooking time: 30 minutes
Serves: 8 slices

Ingredients:

- 4 large egg whites
- 1 teaspoon cornflour
- 1 teaspoon vanilla extract
- 215g caster sugar
- 1 teaspoon white vinegar

Method:

1. Whisk egg white until they form firm peaks.
2. Add the sugar slowly.
3. When mixture is thick and glossy add the cornflour, vinegar and vanilla and mix gently.
4. Line air fryer tray with baking paper and spoon half the mixture onto the paper.
5. Repeat for other half.
6. Air fry each half separately for 30 minutes at 120 degrees Celsius. Serve with berries and whipped cream.

Blooming Onion

Preparation time: 10 minutes
Cooking time: 15 minutes
Serves: 2 people

Ingredients:

- 1 large brown onion
- 60ml milk
- 1 teaspoon of smoked paprika
- 1 teaspoon onion powder
- 1 egg
- 50 g white flour
- 1 teaspoon of garlic powder

Method:

1. Slice the non root side of the onion off.
2. Place cut side down and make 10 slices top to bottom, leaving the base intact. Spread out the segments to create the blooming effect.
3. Beat the egg and add milk then stir.
4. Combine all the dry ingredients in a bowl.
5. Cover onion in the dry ingredients then pour over the egg mixture.
6. Pack the onion with dry ingredients leaving no gaps.
7. Air fry at 180 degrees Celsius for 15 minutes.

Spaghetti and Meatballs

Preparation time: 15 minutes
Cooking time: 15 minutes
Serves: 4 people

Ingredients:

- 2 Large eggs
- 1/4 Teaspoon of salt
- 115 g of breadcrumbs
- 90 g Parmesan cheese
- 230 g of minced beef
- 450g cherry tomatoes
- 190g Marinara sauce
- 2 Teaspoons of Balsamic Vinegar
- 1/4 Teaspoon of black pepper
- 4 cloves of garlic (two chopped and two grated)
- 170 g chopped flat-leaf Parsley
- 340g spaghetti
- 1 Tablespoon of olive oil

Method:

1. Whisk eggs, vinegar, and 1/4 teaspoon of each salt and pepper in a big basin. Add the breadcrumbs, then stir and wait one minute. Garlic, Parmesan, and parsley are all stirred in after that. Add the beef, then blend gently.
2. 20 balls of the beef mixture, each measuring about 1 1/2 inches in diameter, should be formed (balls can touch, but should not be stacked; cook in batches if necessary). Meatballs should be air-fried for 5 minutes at 200 degrees Celsius.
3. Meanwhile, cook spaghetti per package directions.
4. Combine oil, 1/4 teaspoon of salt, and 1/4 teaspoon of pepper in a bowl with the tomatoes and chopped garlic. When the meatballs are thoroughly cooked, scatter them over and continue air-frying for an additional 5 to 6 minutes.
5. Toss spaghetti gently with the meatballs, tomatoes, and marinara. If preferred, garnish with Parmesan and basil before serving.

Air-Fryer Salmon

Preparation time: 5 minutes
Cooking time: 10 minutes
Serves: 4 people

Ingredients:

- 1 teaspoon of salt
- 1 teaspoon of mixed herbs
- 4 salmon fillets
- 1 teaspoon of black pepper
- 1 teaspoon of garlic powder
- 1/2 Tablespoon of olive oil

Method:

1. In a large mixing bowl combine your salt, black pepper, mixed herbs and garlic powder. Mix thoroughly.
2. Next, rub your salmon fillets with olive oil.
3. Afterwards, you can coat your salmon fillets in the mixture of dry ingredients.
4. Place the seasoned salmon fillets in your air fryer basket and cook at 180 degrees Celsius for around ten minutes. If your salmon fillets are larger they may need some extra time so cook for one-minute bursts until they have been cooked through.

Calamari

Preparation time: 5 minutes
Cooking time: 13 minutes
Serves: 4 people

Ingredients:

- 200g calamari rings
- 250g breadcrumbs
- 1/4 teaspoons of salt
- 150g white flour
- 100g heavy whipping cream
- 1/4 teaspoon of black pepper

Method:

1. Pat dry calamari.
2. Mix egg and cream together.
3. Mix dry ingredients together.
4. Stir the salt and pepper into the other dry ingredients.
5. Pour the cream over the calamari then toss in the dry ingredients.
6. Air fry for 13 minutes at 200 degrees Celsius.

Halibut Scampi

Preparation time: 10 minutes
Cooking time: 10 minutes
Serves: 4 people

Ingredients:

- 340g fresh halibut fillet
- 2 tablespoons of butter
- 3 tablespoons white wine
- 1 tablespoon lemon juice
- 2 cloves of garlic
- 1 tablespoon olive oil
- 1/2 teaspoon of salt

Method:

1. Line air fryer tray with tin foil.
2. Cube the fish and place in tray.
3. Cover with melted butter and oil.
4. Sprinkle on the seasonings.
5. Pour the wine over the fish.
6. Air fry for 10 minutes at 200 degrees Celsius.

Lobster Tails

Preparation time: 5 minutes
Cooking time: 8 minutes
Serves: 2 people

Ingredients:

- 2 lobster tails
- 1 tablespoon minced garlic
- 1 teaspoon chopped chives
- 2 tablespoons butter
- 1 teaspoon salt
- 1 teaspoon lemon juice

Method:

1. Combine butter, garlic, salt, chives and lemon juice.
2. Remove lobster tails shell and rest the meat on the top of the shell.
3. Place in air fryer basket and spread butter mixture over the meat.
4. Fry for 4 minutes at 175 degrees Celsius.
5. Spread more butter on the meat and fry for a further 4 minutes.

Wasabi Crab Cakes

Preparation time: 20 minutes
Cooking time: 10 minutes
Serves: 24 cakes

Ingredients:

- 1 medium red pepper, chopped
- 3 green onions, chopped
- 3 tablespoons of mayonnaise
- 1/4 teaspoon of salt
- 100g crabmeat
- 1 celery stalk, chopped
- 2 large egg whites
- 1/4 teaspoon wasabi
- 200g breadcrumbs

Method:

1. Combine the pepper, celery, onions, eggs, mayonnaise, salt and wasabi in a bowl.
2. Carefully mix in the crab meat.
3. Shape into about 24 small patties and coat in breadcrumbs.
4. Cook in batches for 8-12 minutes, turning halfway through at 190 degrees Celsius.

Breaded Shrimp

Preparation time: 5 minutes
Cooking time: 5 minutes
Serves: 2 people

Ingredients:

- 500g cooked and peeled shrimp
- 50g grated parmesan
- 2 beaten eggs
- 250g seasoned breadcrumbs
- 150g oat flour

Method:

1. Mix your breadcrumbs with the cheese.
2. Dip the shrimp into the oat flour then the eggs then the breadcrumbs.
3. Cook for 5 minutes in the air fryer at 200 degrees Celsius.

Tuna Patties

Preparation time: 15 minutes
Cooking time: 10 minutes
Serves: 10 patties

Ingredients:

- 425g canned tuna
- 1 lemon zest
- 55g breadcrumbs
- 3 tablespoons minced onion
- 1/2 teaspoon of garlic powder
- 1/4 teaspoon of salt
- 3 large eggs
- 1 tablespoon lemon juice
- 3 tablespoons grated parmesan
- 1 celery stalk, finely chopped
- 1/2 teaspoon of dried herbs
- 1/4 teaspoon of black pepper

Method:

1. Combine the eggs, lemon zest, lemon juice, breadcrumbs, parmesan, celery, onion and seasonings.
2. Next, fold in the tuna.
3. Scoop up about 25g of the mixture and shape into patties.
4. Cook in batches for 12 minutes, turning halfway. Fry at 170 degrees Celsius.

Brown Sugar Salmon with Garlic

Preparation time: 5 minutes
Cooking time: 10 minutes
Serves: 4 people

Ingredients:

- 500g salmon
- 1/4 teaspoon of black pepper
- 1 teaspoon chilli powder
- 1 teaspoon of Italian seasoning
- 1/4 teaspoons of salt
- 2 tablespoons of brown sugar
- 1/2 teaspoon of smoked paprika
- 1 teaspoon of garlic powder

Method:

1. Combine all of the seasonings in a bowl.
2. Rub your salmon with the seasonings.
3. Cook for 10 minutes skin side down on 200 degrees Celsius.

Fish Fingers

Preparations Time: 10 minutes
Cooking time: 20 minutes
Serves: 4 people

Ingredients:

- 500g cod sliced into fingers
- 1/2 teaspoon of salt
- 2 large eggs, beaten
- 1 teaspoon smoked paprika
- 100g cornstarch
- 1/2 teaspoon of black pepper
- 200g breadcrumbs

Method:

1. Cover your cod fingers in the cornstarch then the egg and finally the breadcrumbs.
2. Arrange on air fryer tray and sprinkle with seasonings.
3. Air fry for 6 minutes at 175 degrees Celsius then turn them over and fry for a further 4-6 minutes.

Seafood Paella

Preparation time: 20 minutes
Cooking time: 40 minutes
Serves: 6 people

Ingredients:

- 1 tablespoon of olive oil
- 100 g chorizo sausage (sliced)
- 1 green pepper, deseeded and roughly chopped
- 4 cloves of garlic, peeled and chopped
- 1 onion, peeled and chopped
- 1/4 teaspoon of salt
- 1/4 teaspoon of black pepper
- 1 pinch of saffron
- 200 g mussels or clams, scrubbed clean and de-bearded
- 300 g paella rice
- 200 gjarred red peppers, drained and roughly chopped
- 400 g chopped tomatoes
- 800 ml chicken stock
- 12 large raw prawns, shell on
- 100 g squid, cleaned and finely sliced into rings
- 150 g green beans, trimmed and finely sliced at an angle
- 2 lemons

Method:

1. Put the temperature at 250 °C. Add the chorizo and olive oil to the pan once it has warmed up. Add the minced green pepper, garlic, onion, parsley stalks, saffron, and a healthy dose of salt and pepper. Cook for 10 minutes.
2. While waiting, sort through the clams or mussels and discard any that are open and don't close when tapped. Rice and canned peppers are added after the temperature is lowered to 175°C. Cook for 5 minutes.
3. Add the stock, canned tomatoes, and a dash of salt. After bringing to a boil, lower the temperature to 130°C. Distribute the prawns, squid, mussels, or clams equally over the top of the paella. Cook for five minutes.
4. After the allotted time has passed, add the green beans that have been cut, cover the pan, and set a timer for an additional 10 minutes.
5. Squeeze the juice from one of the lemons over the paella after roughly chopping and scattering the parsley leaves. Serve with lemon wedges on the side for squeezing over after dividing between bowls.

Salmon Croquettes

Preparation time: 10 minutes
Cooking time: 20 minutes
Serves: 28 croquettes

Ingredients:

- 1kg mashed potatoes
- 100g creamed corn
- 250g aioli
- 2 tablespoons milk
- 50g breadcrumbs
- 300g hot smoked salmon, skinless and flaked
- 1 tablespoon chopped fresh dill
- 1 beaten egg
- 150g white flour

Method:

1. Mix together the mashed potatoes, salmon, corn, dill and 100g aioli in a bowl.
2. Shape into croquettes.
3. Whisk together the egg and milk.
4. Dip the croquettes into the flour then the egg and finally the breadcrumbs.
5. Air fry for 10 minutes at 180 degrees Celsius.

Prawn Sesame Balls

Preparation time: 45 minutes
Cooking time: 15 minutes
Serves: 18 balls

Ingredients:

- 250g frozen prawns, thawed
- 2cm piece grated fresh ginger
- 1/2 teaspoon caster sugar
- 1 teaspoons sesame oil
- 2 beaten eggs
- 3 unsliced brioche hotdog buns
- 2 chopped garlic cloves
- 1 egg white
- 2 teaspoons soy sauce
- 1 sliced green shallot
- 150g sesame seeds

Method:

1. Blend the prawns, garlic, ginger, egg white, sugar, soy sauce, shallot and sesame oil in a food processor.
2. Place in the fridge for 30 minutes.
3. Place 1/2 tablespoon amount of the prawn mixture onto brioche slices.
4. Dip into the egg then roll in sesame seeds.
5. Fry in batches for 6 minutes at 170 degrees Celsius.

Coconut Prawns

Preparation time: 5 minutes
Cooking time: 30 minutes
Serves: 4 people

Ingredients:

- 65g white flour
- 1/4 teaspoon of black pepper
- 2 beaten eggs
- 35g shredded coconut
- 1/4 teaspoon of salt
- 100g breadcrumbs
- 450g large prawns peeled and de-veined.

Method:

1. Season the flour with salt and pepper.
2. Mix the breadcrumbs with the coconut.
3. Dip prawns in the flour then the egg and finally the breadcrumbs.
4. Air fry at 200 degrees Celsius for 10-12 minutes.

Fried Catfish

Preparation time: 5 minutes
Cooking time: 20 minutes
Serves: 4 people

Ingredients:

- 4 catfish fillets
- 1/4 teaspoon of salt
- 1 tablespoon chopped parsley
- 1 tablespoon olive oil
- 1/4 teaspoon of black pepper

Method:

1. Pat your catfish fillets dry.
2. Rub with the oil and seasonings.
3. Cook in batches for 20 minutes, turning halfway through on 200 degrees Celsius.

Goulash Style Stew

Preparation time: 15 minutes
Cooking time: 45 minutes
Serves: 4 people

Ingredients:

- 500g cubed pork or beef or 250g of each
- 25g chorizo or Hungarian salami
- 1 tomato (diced)
- 150ml water
- 1 teaspoon of smoked paprika
- 1/4 teaspoon of salt
- 1 carrot (sliced)
- 20g tomato puree
- 1 white onion
- 5 mushrooms (diced)
- 1 red pepper (diced)
- 1 beef or pork stock cube
- 1/4 teaspoon of garlic powder
- 1/4 teaspoon of black pepper
- 3 rashers of bacon (finely chopped)

Method:

1. Preheat your air fryer at 200 degrees Celsius.
2. Combine all of your ingredients and let sit for around 10 minutes.
3. Place in the air fryer tray and cook for 45 minutes.

Lamb Chops

Preparation time: 5 minutes
Cooking time: 10 minutes
Serves: 4 people

Ingredients:

- 8 pre cut lamb chops
- 2 teaspoons of rosemary
- 1 teaspoon of minced garlic
- 1/2 teaspoon of black pepper
- 2 tablespoons of olive oil
- 2 teaspoons of thyme
- 1/2 teaspoon of salt

Method:

1. Mix together the oil, rosemary, thyme, garlic, salt and pepper.
2. Gently toss the lamb chops into the seasoned oil and rub into the meat.
3. Air fry at 190 degrees Celsius for 10 minutes, turning halfway and let rest for 5 minutes before serving.

Ham Steaks

Preparation time 5 minutes
Cooking time: 8 minutes
Serves: 4 people

Ingredients:

- 2 ham steaks
- 50g sour cream
- 20g cream cheese
- 1/4 teaspoon of salt
- 2 tablespoons of maple syrup
- 20g mayonnaise
- 1 teaspoon chives
- 1/4 teaspoon of pepper

Method:

1. Preheat your air fryer to 200 degrees Celsius.
2. Spray the air fryer tray with non stick cooking spray.
3. Brush the maple syrup all over the ham steaks.
4. Air fry for 8 minutes, turning halfway.
5. Combine the mayonnaise, cream cheese, chives, sour cream, salt and pepper and serve as a sauce.

Pork and Apple Sausage Rolls

Preparation time: 25 minutes
Cooking time: 35 minutes
Serves: 18 rolls

Ingredients:

- 500g pork mince
- 100g grated cheddar
- 2 tablespoons of chopped flat leaf parsley
- 2 eggs, beaten
- 2 teaspoons fennel seeds
- 1 peeled and grated apple
- 2 chopped green onions
- 2 teaspoon of fresh thyme leaves
- 3 sheets of frozen puff pastry, thawed
- 2 teaspoons sesame seeds

Method:

1. Combine the mince, apple, cheddar, onion, garlic, thyme, parsley and half of the egg.
2. Place one pastry sheet on to a flat surface and cut in half. Fill one half with the mince mixture and roll up the pastry to form a sausage roll.
3. Brush with the remaining egg, score lines down the rolls and top with fennel and sesame seeds.
4. Cook for 10-12 minutes at 200 degrees Celsius.

Pastry Pork Hot Dogs

Preparation time: 10 minutes

Cooking time: 14 minutes
Serves: 8 hot dogs

Ingredients:

- 8 pork hot dogs
- 8 slice of cheese
- 1 tablespoon butter
- 1/4 teaspoon of pepper
- 1 package of frozen puff pastry, thawed
- 2 onions, finely chopped
- 1/4 teaspoon of salt

Method:

1. Fry your onions in a frying pan along with the salt, pepper and butter.
2. When the onions are browned and softened, remove from the heat and let cool.
3. Slice your puff pastry into 8 strips.
4. Lay a slice of cheese on each strip of pastry.
5. Place a generous helping of onions on top of the cheese.
6. Lay a sausage on each piece of pastry.
7. Carefully wrap each strip around each sausage.
8. You can add a layer of ketchup or mustard between the sausage and the pastry if you would like to.
9. Air fry for 12-14 minutes at 180 degrees Celsius or until the pastry is golden brown.

Lamb Skewers

Preparation time: 10 minutes
Cooking time: 15 minutes
Serves 2 people

Ingredients:

- 500g lamb chopped into cubes
- 1/4 teaspoon of black pepper
- 1/2 teaspoon of rosemary
- 1/4 teaspoon of salt
- 1/2 teaspoon of thyme
- 2 tablespoons of olive oil

Method:

1. Place the lamb cubes along wooden skewers.
2. Combine your seasonings with the olive oil and gently brush over the lamb skewers.
3. Cook in batches of about 4 per batch.
4. Air fry for 12-15 minutes at 190 degrees Celsius or until the lamb is cooked through.

Teriyaki Pork

Preparation time: 5 minutes
Cooking time: 15 minutes
Serves: 4 people

Ingredients:

- 4 pork chops
- 100ml teriyaki marinade
- 1/4 teaspoon of salt
- 2 tablespoons of horseradish sauce
- 1/4 teaspoon of ground cinnamon
- 1/4 teaspoon of black pepper

Method:

1. Mix the teriyaki marinade together with the horseradish, salt, pepper and cinnamon.
2. Pour all over your pork chops making sure they are thoroughly coated in the marinade.
3. Let sit for around 30 minutes.
4. Heat air fryer to 200 degrees and air fry the pork for about 15 minutes, turning halfway through.

Barbecue Ribs

Preparation time: 5 minutes
Cooking time: 25 minutes
Serves: 4 people

Ingredients:

- Rack of pork ribs cut in half
- 1 1/2 teaspoons garlic powder
- 4 tablespoons of barbecue sauce
- 1 teaspoon smoked paprika
- 2 teaspoon of ground black pepper
- 1 tablespoon of honey

Methods:

1. Combine your seasonings in a large bowl.
2. Pat your pork ribs dry with a paper towel.
3. Line the air fryer tray with baking paper or foil.
4. Cover your ribs generously with the seasoning.
5. Air fry each half separately for 20 minutes at 190 degrees Celsius.
6. Brush extra barbecue sauce on the ribs and fry for a further 2 minutes.

Meatloaf

Preparation time: 10 minutes
Cooking time: 25 minutes
Serves: 8 people

Ingredients:

- 750g minced beef
- 200g crushed Ritz biscuits
- 1/2 medium onion, chopped
- 1 can of diced tomatoes
- 1/2 teaspoon pepper
- 2 large eggs
- 25ml milk
- 50g red pepper chopped
- 1 teaspoon of salt

Method:

1. Combine all of your ingredients into a large bowl and mix thoroughly using your hands.
2. Line your air fryer tray with baking paper.
3. Shape the meatloaf on the air fryer tray.
4. Cook in the air fryer at 190 degrees Celsius for 18-20 minutes or until cooked through.

Taco Casserole

Preparation time: 10 minutes
Cooking time: 20 minutes
Serves: 4 people
Ingredients:

- 500g ground beef
- 50ml water
- 200g diced tomatoes
- 50g sour cream
- 100g grated cheddar
- 3 tablespoons of taco seasoning
- 100g chopped red pepper
- 4 large eggs
- 75g heavy cream

Method:

1. Start by browning the meat in a frying pan.
2. Add water, taco seasoning, pepper and the tomatoes to the pan and simmer for 3 minutes.
3. Preheat the air fryer to 175 degrees Celsius.
4. Mix eggs, sour cream and the cream.
5. Line the air fryer pan with the meat mixture and top with the egg mixture.
6. Cover with the grated cheese.
7. Air fry for 18 minutes then take out, add extra cheese and air fry for a final 2 minutes.

Garlic Steak Bites

Preparation time: 5 minutes
Cooking time: 10 minutes
Serves: 6 people
Ingredients:

- 1.5kg beef steak chopped into cubes
- 1 teaspoon of ground black pepper
- 1/4 teaspoon of salt
- 2 tablespoons of garlic powder
- 1 teaspoon of olive oil

Method:

1. Mix the garlic powder with the black pepper, salt and olive oil.
2. Toss the steak pieces in the seasoning and sprinkle with a little extra salt.
3. Place in air fryer basket and spray with non stick cooking spray.
4. Cook for 10 minutes, tossing halfway through at 200 degrees Celsius.

Pork Belly Bites

Preparation time: 10 minutes
Cooking time: 40 minutes
Serves: 4 people

Ingredients:

- 1kg pork belly
- 3cm knob of ginger, peeled and sliced
- 100g caster sugar
- 1/4 teaspoon of salt
- 250ml orange juice
- 2 star anise
- 2 tablespoons of soy sauce

Method:

1. Cut the pork belly into 4cm cubes.
2. Sprinkle with salt and place in the air fryer.
3. Fry for 15 minutes at 200 degrees Celsius.
4. Combine the rest of the ingredients in a saucepan and mix until the sugar has dissolved.
5. Pour over the pork and serve.

Flank Steak

Preparation time: 5 minutes
Cooking time: 15 minutes
Serves: 4 people

Ingredients:

- 500g flank steak
- 1/2 teaspoon of black pepper
- 1 teaspoon of smoked paprika
- 1 teaspoon of salt
- 1 teaspoon of garlic powder

Method:

1. Combine all of the dry ingredients in a bowl.
2. Dry meat with a paper towel.
3. Using a meat hammer, tenderise the meat.
4. Rub the seasoning into the meat thoroughly.
5. Air fry the steaks for 8 minutes, turning halfway through at 190 degrees Celsius.
6. Air fry for a couple of extra minutes if you prefer your steak well done.

Beef Wellington

Preparation time: 40 minutes
Cooking time: 40 minutes
Serves: 2 people

Ingredients:

- 1 tablespoon olive oil
- 200g button mushrooms, chopped
- 2 crushed garlic cloves
- 2 teaspoons mustard
- 1 egg, beaten
- 2 x 150g beef steaks
- 2 shallots, peeled and chopped
- 7 slices prosciutto
- 1 sheet frozen puff pastry, thawed

Method:

1. Cook steak in a frying pan for 3-4 minutes.
2. Then fry the mushrooms, shallots and garlic for 15 minutes.
3. Lay 6 of the prosciutto slices on cling film and spread over the mushroom mixture.
4. Then cover the mixture with the two steaks.
5. Spread the steaks with mustard.
6. Lay the final prosciutto slice over the mustard.
7. Roll up the steaks in the prosciutto wrapped in clingfilm and place in the fridge.
8. Lay the pastry on a flat surface and unwrap the clingfilm from the steaks.
9. Wrap the steaks in the pastry.
10. Brush the top with the egg and score diagonal lines across the pastry.
11. Place seam side down in the air fryer basket.
12. Air fry for 20 minutes at 180 degrees Celsius.

Roast Pork Belly

Preparation time: 5 minutes
Cooking time: 55 minutes
Serves: 4 people

Ingredients:

- 1kg pork belly
- olive oil spray
- 1 tablespoon of butter
- 1 teaspoon of honey
- 2 teaspoon sea salt
- 1/4 teaspoon of black pepper
- 1 teaspoon of sugar

Method:

1. Dry the pork with a paper towel and rub all over with the salt, pepper and oil.
2. Cook in air fryer at 200 degrees Celsius for 25 minutes.
3. Then reduce the heat to 160 degrees Celsius and cook for a further 30 minutes.
4. Meanwhile, combine the butter, sugar and honey in a saucepan and melt on a medium heat.
   For the final five minutes of Cooking time, brush the pork with the glaze.

Delicious Crispy Sweet Potato Fries

Preparation time: 5 minutes
Cooking time: 45 minutes
Serves: 2 people

Ingredients:

- 2 sweet potatoes
- 1 teaspoon of barbecue seasoning
- 1/4 teaspoon of salt
- 1 teaspoon of olive oil
- 1/2 teaspoon mixed herbs
- 1/4 teaspoon of black pepper

Method:

1. Slice the sweet potatoes into 1/2 cm sticks after peeling. Place them in a dish, add the oil, and toss well to coat. Salt, pepper, mixed herbs, and barbecue seasoning should be added before giving everything a good mix with your hands to ensure that everything is uniformly coated.
2. Cook, in batches, in a single layer in your air fryer basket at 180C for approximately 10-15 minutes, or until gently browned, shaking or tossing every 5 minutes. Return the fries to the air fryer once each batch has finished cooking, give it a good shake, and cook for an additional one to two minutes to heat through.

Butternut Squash Wedges

Preparation time: 10 minutes
Cooking time: 15 minutes
Serves: 4 people

Ingredients:

- 1 butternut squash
- olive oil spray
- 1/4 teaspoon of black pepper
- 1/4 teaspoon of thyme
- 2 teaspoons of all spice
- 1/4 teaspoon of salt
- 1/4 teaspoon of oregano
- 1/4 teaspoon of rosemary

Method:

1. Peel the butternut squash and slice into wedges like you would with potato wedges.
2. Spray the air fryer basket with the oil spray.
3. Add the squash to the basket and spray with the oil spray.
4. Shake the squash to evenly distribute the oil.
5. Sprinkle the all spice, salt, pepper, oregano, thyme and rosemary all over the squash.
6. Air fry for 15 minutes at 190 degrees Celsius, turning halfway through.

Corn on the Cob

Preparation time: 5 minutes
Cooking time: 12 minutes
Serves: 4 people

Ingredients:

- 4 full piece of corn on the cob
- 1/4 teaspoon of black pepper
- 4 teaspoons of butter
- 1/4 teaspoon of salt
- 2 table spoons of olive oil

Method:

1. Combine the oil, salt and pepper.
2. Brush all four piece of corn with the oil and seasoning.
3. Place the corn in the air fryer and fry at 180 degrees Celsius for 12 minutes, turning halfway.
4. When the corn is finished, add the butter.

Onion Rings

Preparation time: 10 minutes
Cooking time: 40 minutes
Serves: 4 people

Ingredients:

- 3 medium sized yellow onions
- 2 tablespoons cornstarch
- 1 teaspoon of black pepper
- 150ml milk
- Nonstick cooking spray
- 200g white flour
- 1 teaspoon of salt
- 3 large eggs
- 600g breadcrumbs

Method:

1. Slice the root off of the onions and cut into 1/2 inch thick rings.
2. Combine the flour, salt and pepper in one bowl.
3. In another bowl, whisk the eggs and milk together.
4. In a third bowl you can put your breadcrumbs.
5. Dip each onion rig in the flour then the eggs and finally the breadcrumbs.
6. You can place the onion rings into your air fryer tray after spraying the tray with non stick cooking spray.
7. Air fry your onion rings at 180 degrees Celsius for five minutes, flip then fry for another five minutes.

Air Fryer Baked Potatoes

Preparation time: 5 minutes
Cooking time: 35 minutes
Serves: 2 people

Ingredients:

- 2 baking potatoes
- 1/4 teaspoon of black pepper
- 1 can of baked beans (optional)
- 2 tablespoons olive oil
- 1/4 teaspoon of salt
- 50g grated cheese (optional)

Method:

1. Pierce your potatoes all over with a fork.
2. Coat your potatoes in olive oil.
3. Roll the potatoes in the seasoning and rub to distribute evenly.
4. Air fry at 180 degrees Celsius for 35 minutes.
5. Add the beans topped with cheese in a ramekin to the air fryer and cook with the potatoes for the final five minutes.

Delicious Paprika Halloumi

Preparation time: 2 minutes
Cooking time: 15 minutes
Serves: 3 people

Ingredients:

- 225g of halloumi
- 1 teaspoon of smoked paprika
- 1/4 teaspoon of black pepper
- 1/4 teaspoon of garlic powder
- 1 tablespoon of maple syrup
- 1 teaspoon of olive oil
- 1/4 teaspoon of salt
- 1/4 teaspoon of onion powder
- 1 tablespoon of butter
- 1 tablespoon of caster sugar

Method:

1. Preheat your air fryer to 200 degrees Celcius for two minutes.
2. Take your halloumi and cut it into 1cm thick slices. Then pat the halloumi dry with kitchen paper.
3. Next, rub your halloumi with the olive oil and sprinkle the seasonings over the top of the slices.
4. Place in your air fryer basket and cook for eight minutes then turn over and flip for a further two minutes or until the halloumi is golden brown on the edges.
5. For a sweet glaze combine the butter, sugar and maple syrup in a saucepan on medium heat until the sugar has dissolved.
6. Coat the halloumi with the glaze for the final two minutes.

Air Fried Bacon-Roasted Potatoes

Preparation time: 10 minutes

Cooking time: 20 minutes

Serves: 4 people

Ingredients:

- 640g new potatoes
- 1 tablespoon of olive oil
- 1/4 tablespoon of black pepper
- 3 medium shallots
- 1/2 tablespoon of mustard
- 4 sprigs of Thyme
- 1/4 tablespoon of salt
- 3 rashers of bacon
- 1 tablespoon of balsamic vinegar

Method:

1. Quartered potatoes, thyme sprigs, oil, 1/2 teaspoon salt, and 1/4 teaspoon pepper should be combined in a large bowl. Add to the air fryer and add bacon on top. For 6 to 12 minutes, air-fry bacon at 200 degrees Celsius until it is crisp. Place the bacon on a paper towel and let it cool before cutting it into pieces.
2. After 8 minutes of air-frying, shake the potatoes. Add the shallots to the basket with the potatoes, toss to incorporate, and air-fry for 8 to 12 minutes, or until the vegetables are soft and golden brown.
3. In the meantime, combine the vinegar, mustard, and thyme leaves in a large bowl. Fold in bacon after adding any oils from the bottom of the basket and transferring the cooked vegetables to the bowl.

Maple Glazed Coriander Carrots

Preparation time: 20 minutes

Cooking time: 25 minutes

Serves: 4 people

Ingredients:

- 680g carrots
- 1 1/2 teaspoons of crushed whole coriander seeds
- 1/4 teaspoon of black pepper
- 1 teaspoon of lime zest
- 1 1/2 tablespoon olive oil
- 1/4 teaspoon of salt
- 1 tablespoon of maple syrup
- 1 teaspoon of lime juice

Method:

1. Preheat your air fryer to 210 degrees Celcius.
2. Add carrots to the air fryer tray along with 1 tablespoon of oil, 1/4 teaspoon each of salt and pepper, and coriander.
3. Roast for 20 to 25 minutes total, flipping after 15 minutes, until golden brown and soft. Add maple syrup, lime juice, zest, and the final 1/2 tbsp oil right away.

Mashed Potatoes

Preparation time: 10 minutes
Cooking time: 25 minutes
Serves: 4 people

Ingredients:

- 900g baking potatoes
- 50g cream cheese
- 1/4 teaspoon of black pepper
- 2 tablespoons of butter
- 1/4 teaspoon of salt
- 2 stalks of fresh chives

Method:

1. Quarter your potatoes and place inside foil then cook in your air fryer at 200 degrees Celsius for 25 minutes.
2. Next mash them thoroughly and add your butter and cream cheese.
3. Finely chop your chives and add to the potatoes.

Garlic Green Beans

Preparation time: 5 minutes
Cooking time: 10 minutes
Serves: 4 people

Ingredients:

- 100g green beans
- 1/4 teaspoons of salt
- 2 table spoons of olive oil
- 1/4 teaspoon of garlic powder
- 1/4 teaspoon of black pepper
- 50g bacon lardons (optional)

Method:

1. Wash your green beans and remove the ends.
2. Coat your green beans in the oil.
3. Toss the oiled beans in the seasoning.
4. Place the green beans into your air fryer tray.
5. Add your bacon lardons if choosing to.
6. Air fry at 180 degrees Celsius for 8-10 minutes, shaking halfway through.

Roasted Veggie Cubes with Bacon

Preparation time: 10 minutes
Cooking time: 25 minutes
Serves: 4 people

Ingredients:

- 3 baking potatoes
- 2 carrots

- 2 parsnips
- 1/4 teaspoon of salt
- 2 tablespoons of olive oil
- 1/4 teaspoon of oregano
- 100g bacon lardons
- 1/4 teaspoon of pepper
- 1/4 teaspoon of rosemary

Method:

1. Preheat your air fryer to 200 degrees Celsius.
2. Cube all of your vegetable and place in air fryer tray.
3. Add your bacon lardons to the air fryer tray.
4. Drizzle with the oil and add your seasonings then mix thoroughly.
5. Air fry for 25 minutes.

Air Fryer Asparagus

Preparation time: 5 minutes
Cooking time: 10 minutes
Serves: 4 people

Ingredients:

- 500g fresh asparagus with trimmed ends
- 1/4 teaspoon of salt
- 1/4 teaspoon of rosemary
- 2 teaspoons of olive oil
- 1/4 teaspoon of black pepper

Method:

1. After washing and trimming your asparagus, coat with olive oil.
2. Season your oiled asparagus with rosemary, salt and pepper.
3. Set your air fryer to 180 degrees Celsius.
4. Fry for 7-10 minutes, shaking and turning halfway through.

Hasselback Potatoes

Preparation time: 10 minutes
Cooking time: 35 minutes
Serves: 2 people

Ingredients:

- 2 large russet potatoes
- 2 teaspoons of salt
- 2 tablespoons of olive oil
- 1/4 teaspoon of black pepper.
- 4 rashers of bacon, chopped (optional)

Method:

1. Slice both potatoes almost all the way through leaving about 1/4 inch at the bottom. Placing

the potatoes between two chopsticks can help keep the cuts neat.

2. Drizzle your potatoes with olive oil and add some salt.

3. Bake at 150 degrees Celsius in the air fryer for 15 minutes.

4. Remove and drizzle with more oil and salt and pepper.

5. Bake for a further 15 minutes. Add your bacon now if you are using bacon.

6. Drizzle with oil and salt again and bake for a final 5 minutes.

Air Fryer Buffalo Style Cauliflower

Preparation time: 2 minutes
Cooking time: 12 minutes
Serves: 2 people

Ingredients:

- 1 large floret of cauliflower
- 1/2 teaspoon of Worcestershire sauce
- 1/2 teaspoon of vinegar
- 1 teaspoon of hot sauce
- 1 teaspoon of butter

Method:

1. Melt the butter and add the hot sauce, Worcestershire sauce and vinegar.

2. Cut your broccoli and place in the air fryer tray.

3. Air fry at 200 degrees Celsius for 7-9 minutes.

4. Take out and add your sauce.

5. Air fry for a further 3 minutes.

Stuffed Chicken in the Air Fryer

Preparation time: 15 minutes

Cooking time: 10 minutes

Serves: 4 people

Ingredients:

- 4 Chicken Breasts
- 4 Tablespoons of Goats Cheese
- 4 slices of Proscuitto
- 4 Tablespoons of pesto
- 1 1/2 Tablespoons of olive oil
- 2 cloves of minced garlic

Method:

1. Each chicken breast should have a pocket that is as broad as feasible without cutting through, so insert a knife into the thickest section of each breast and slide it back and forth.
2. Using a spoon, distribute the goat cheese and pesto among the pockets. Rub in the remaining 1/2 tbsp of oil and season with salt and pepper.
3. Slices of prosciutto are laid out on a cutting board. Chicken is then placed on top, wrapped in prosciutto, and placed seam-side down in an air fryer basket.
4. Air fry for ten minutes at 190 degrees Celcius.

Turkey Legs

Preparation time: 5 minutes

Cooking time: 25 minutes

Serves: 2 people

Ingredients:

- 2 large turkey legs
- 1/2 teaspoon of smoked paprika
- 1/2 teaspoon of thyme
- 1/2 teaspoon of sage
- 2 tablespoons of melted butter
- 1/2 teaspoon of salt
- 1/2 teaspoon of rosemary
- 1/4 teaspoon of black pepper

Method:

1. Combine all of the seasonings with the melted butter.
2. Brush your flavoured butter all over the turkey legs.
3. Place turkey legs into your air fryer tray.
4. Air fry for 25-30 minutes at 200 degrees Celsius.

Fabulous Chicken Taquitos

Preparation time: 15 minutes

Cooking time: 15 minutes

Serves: 5 people

Ingredients:

- 115g of cream cheese
- 90g Sour cream
- 1/4 teaspoon of black pepper
- 170g of cheddar cheese
- Olive oil

- 113g Red Pasta Sauce
- 1/4 teaspoon of salt
- 1/2 a chicken shredded
- 12 Small tortillas

Method:

1. Start by brushing your air fryer tray with oil and preheating it at 200 degrees Celcius.
2. Mix the cream cheese, sour cream, pasta sauce, and 1/4 teaspoon each of salt and pepper in a large bowl. Cheddar cheese and chicken are combined into the mixture.
3. Place tortillas in batches on a microwave-safe dish, then cover them with a wet paper towel. Microwave for 30 to 60 seconds, or until warm and malleable.
4. Distribute the mixture among tortillas, roll them up tightly, and set seam sides down on the air fryer tray that has been prepared. Brush with oil and bake for 12 to 15 minutes, or until golden brown and crisp.
5. Serve hot with a selection of dips!

Sticky Chicken Bites

Preparation time: 15 minutes
Cooking time: 25 minutes
Serves: 4 people

Ingredients:

- 70g white flour
- 1/2 teaspoon garlic powder
- 50g cornflour
- 500g chicken breast chopped into small pieces
- 2 tablespoons sweet chilli sauce
- 40g chopped butter

- 1/2 teaspoon salt
- 2 teaspoons smoked paprika powder
- 2 eggs
- 75g barbecue sauce
- 2 tablespoons honey

Method:

1. Combine the flour, salt, garlic, onion and paprika.
2. Place corn flour in another bowl.
3. Beat eggs in a third bowl.
4. Dip the chicken in the flour mix then the eggs then the cornflour.
5. Air fry chicken in two batches for 10 minutes each at 180 degrees Celsius.
6. Combine remaining ingredients and warm in a saucepan for 2 to 3 minutes until the butter has melted.
7. Pour sauce over chicken and serve.

Popcorn Chicken

Preparation time: 10 minutes
Cooking time: 10 minutes
Serves: 4 people

Ingredients:

- 2 chicken breasts
- 200g breadcrumbs
- 1 teaspoon of salt
- 1 teaspoon of smoked paprika
- 1/2 teaspoon of olive oil spray
- 200g flour
- 2 eggs, beaten
- 1 teaspoon of black pepper
- 1/4 teaspoon of cayenne pepper

Method:

1. Preheat air fryer to 200 degrees Celsius.
2. Pat dry the chicken.
3. Cut the chicken into popcorn bite sized pieces.
4. Place the flour and eggs into separate bowls.
5. In another bowl combine the seasonings and breadcrumbs.
6. Dip the chicken into flour, then egg then finally breadcrumbs and place in air fryer tray.
7. Spray with the spray olive oil.
8. Air fry for 10 minutes, shaking halfway through.

Turkey Burgers

Preparation time: 5 minutes
Cooking time: 10 minutes
Serves: 4 people

Ingredients:

- 500g minced turkey
- 200g shredded mozzarella
- 100g breadcrumbs
- 1/2 teaspoon of salt
- 1/2 teaspoon of rosemary
- 1/2 teaspoon of sage
- 1 large egg, beaten
- 100g finely chopped onion
- 1 teaspoon minced garlic
- 1/4 teaspoon of black pepper
- 1/2 teaspoon of thyme

Method:

1. Preheat your air fryer to 180 degrees Celsius.
2. Combine all of your ingredients into a bowl and mix well.
3. Divide the mixture into four.
4. Shape into four burgers.
5. Air fry for 10 minutes in two batches, turning halfway through.

Coconut Chicken

Preparation time: 5 minutes
Cooking time: 12 minutes
Serves: 4 people

Ingredients:

- 500g cubed chicken
- 100g coconut flour
- 1/2 teaspoon of salt
- 250g coconut flakes
- 3 large eggs, beaten
- 1 teaspoon smoked paprika
- 1/2 teaspoon of black pepper
- 200g breadcrumbs

Method:

1. Pat your chicken dry.
2. Combine the coconut flakes with the breadcrumbs in one bowl.
3. In another bowl mix the seasonings with the coconut flour.
4. Dip the chicken in the coconut flour then the egg and finally the breadcrumbs.
5. Air fry for 12 minutes, tossing halfway through at 190 degrees Celsius.

Chicken Casserole

Preparation time: 10 minutes
Cooking time: 4 minutes
Serves: 4 people

Ingredients:

- 200g egg noodles
- 400g broccoli florets
- 200 g cheddar cheese, grated
- 100 g sour cream
- 1/2 teaspoon of black pepper
- 400g rotisserie chicken
- 4 tablespoons of butter
- 1 can of cream of chicken soup
- 1 teaspoon of salt

Method:

1. Prepare your noodles on the stove.
2. Once finished cooking, drain the noodles and add your chicken and broccoli to the saucepan.
3. Next, add the butter, cheese, soup, sour cream, salt and pepper. Stir very well.
4. Smooth the casserole into your air fryers casserole dish attachment or pizza pan.
5. Air fry at 180 degrees Celsius for 4-6 minutes.

Chicken Burgers

Preparation time: 5 minutes
Cooking time: 10 minutes
Serves: 4 people

Ingredients:

- 500g minced chicken
- 200g shredded mozzarella
- 100g breadcrumbs
- 1/2 teaspoon of salt
- 1 large egg, beaten
- 100g finely chopped onion
- 1 teaspoon minced garlic
- 1/4 teaspoon of black pepper

Method:

1. Preheat your air fryer to 180 degrees Celsius.
2. Combine all of your ingredients into a bowl and mix well.
3. Divide the mixture into four.
4. Shape into four burgers.
5. Air fry for 10 minutes in two batches, turning halfway through.

Simple Chicken Wings

Preparation time: 5 minutes
Cooking time: 35 minutes
Serves: 4 people

Ingredients:

- 1kg chicken wings
- 1/2 teaspoon of salt
- 1/2 teaspoon of garlic powder
- 1 tablespoon of olive oil
- 1/2 teaspoon of pepper
- 1/2 teaspoon of smoked paprika

Method:

1. Use a pair of sharp kitchen scissors to cut each chicken wing in half at the joint. You may choose to leave the wing tips on if you want. Chicken wings should not overlap as they are placed into an air fryer tray after being coated with oil and seasoning.
2. Set the air fryer to cook at 200 degrees Celsius for 35 minutes. The wings should be nearly falling off the bone when they are soft and cooked through. If not, heat for an additional 5 minutes. Any extra chicken fat should have dropped off into the fryer's base by the time the skin bubbled and became crispy. Avoid leaving the chicken in the fryer for too long because the steam will make the skin re-soften. Immediately pour into a bowl and offer dipping sauce.

Sweet and Sour Chicken

Preparation time: 5 minutes
Cooking time: 18 minutes
Serves: 4 people

Ingredients:

- 500 g chicken cut into strips
- 50 ml white wine vinegar
- 25ml pineapple juice
- 50g cornstarch
- 1 tablespoon of soy sauce
- 25ml water
- 100g sugar
- 1 teaspoon garlic minced
- 2 tablespoons cornstarch

Method:

1. Cut the chicken into cubes and coat in cornstarch.
2. Preheat the air fryer to 190 degrees Celsius.
3. Cook the chicken for 18 minutes, turning halfway through.
4. Combine the other ingredients into a saucepan and heat until the sugar has dissolved.
5. When the chicken is cooked, toss in the sauce and serve.

Dorito Chicken

Preparation time:15 minutes
Cooking time: 12 minutes
Serves: 4 people

Ingredients:

- 500 g chicken breast
- 1/2 teaspoon of salt
- 1 large beaten egg
- 1 teaspoon garlic powder
- 1/2 teaspoon of black pepper
- 1 bag of cheese Doritos, crushed

Method:

1. Pat dry your chicken breasts.
2. Dip into the beaten egg.
3. Combine the Doritos with the seasonings and roll the chicken breasts into the mixture.
4. Air fry for 12 minutes, turning halfway at 200 degrees Celsius.

Honey BBQ Chicken Legs

Preparation time: 10 minutes
Cooking time: 35 minutes
Serves: 4 people

Ingredients:

- 1kg chicken legs
- 1/2 teaspoon of salt
- 1/2 teaspoon of garlic powder
- 3 tablespoons of honey
- 2 tablespoons of soy sauce
- 1 tablespoon of olive oil
- 1/2 teaspoon of pepper
- 1/2 teaspoon of smoked paprika
- 4 tablespoons bbq sauce

Method:

1. Combine your bbq sauce, honey and soy sauce then mix well.
2. Add all your dry seasonings and olive oil to the bbq soy sauce and combine thoroughly.
3. Using a pastry brush, coat the outside of your chicken legs in the honey bbq seasoning.
4. Set the air fryer to cook at 200 degrees Celsius for 35 minutes. The legs should be nearly falling off the bone when they are soft and cooked through. If not, heat for an additional 5 minutes. Any extra chicken fat should have dropped off into the fryer's base by the time the skin bubbled and became crispy. Avoid leaving the chicken in the fryer for too long because the steam will make the skin re-soften. Immediately pour into a bowl and offer dipping sauce.

Crunchy Chick Pea Snacks

Preparation time: 5 minutes

Cooking time: 30 minutes

Serves: 2 people

Ingredients:

- 2 cans of chickpeas
- 1/4 tablespoon of salt
- 1/4 teaspoon of smoked paprika
- 2 tablespoons of olive oil
- 1/4 tablespoon of black pepper
- 1/4 teaspoon of garlic powder

Method:

1. Dry the chickpeas thoroughly with paper towels after rinsing and draining them. Discard any loose skins.
2. Add salt, pepper, garlic, smoked paprika and olive oil to an air fryer tray. Roast for 30 minutes, stirring the pan occasionally, at 210 degrees Celsius until crisp.
3. Take out of the air fryer and place in a bowl; season to taste. As they cool, chickpeas will continue to crisp.

Vegetable Crisps

Preparation time: 10 minutes

Cooking time: 35 minutes

Serves: 4 people

Ingredients:

- 3 potato peels
- 1 carrot peel
- 1/4 teaspoon of black pepper
- 1 sweet potato peel
- 30 g sea salt flakes
- 1/4 teaspoon of smoked paprika

Method:

1. Preheat your air fryer to 70 degrees Celsius.
2. Place your vegetable peel into the air fryer basket.
3. Air fry for 10 minutes.
4. Toss in the sea salt flakes.
5. Air fry for a final 15 minutes until crispy.
6. Toss in the black pepper and paprika and serve!

Cauliflower Cheese Bites

Preparation time: 20 minutes

Cooking time: 12 minutes

Serves: 2 people

Ingredients:

- 2 eggs
- 40g grated parmesan
- 1 teaspoon garlic powder
- 20g butter
- 125 g sour cream
- 50g breadcrumbs
- 2 teaspoons smoked paprika
- 450 g cauliflower, cut into smaller florets
- 2 crushed garlic cloves
- 130 g cheddar cheese or mozzarella

Method:

1. Whisk the eggs and in a separate bowl combine the breadcrumbs, parmesan and seasonings.
2. Dip the cauliflower in the egg then the breadcrumbs.
3. Place the cauliflower into air fryer tray and fry at 180 degrees Celsius for 12 minutes.
4. Melt the butter in a saucepan and add the garlic. Then stir in the sour cream and cheese. Cook for 2 or 3 minutes until all the cheese has melted.
5. Pour cheese sauce over the cauliflower and serve.

Pao de Quejio (Brazilian Cheese Bread)

Preparation time: 20 minutes
Cooking time: 1 hour 15 minutes
Serves: 32 cheese bread puffs

Ingredients:

- 250 ml whole milk
- 300g tapioca flour
- 70g grated parmesan
- 125 ml vegetable oil
- 2 eggs

Method:

1. Heat the milk and oil in a saucepan for 2 minutes.
2. Add the flour and stir.
3. Mix for 2 minutes and let cool slightly.
4. Add the eggs and beat thoroughly.
5. Next, add the cheese.
6. Use damp hands to shape into small balls.
7. Spray air fryer tray with non stick cooking spray.
8. Place balls in the tray and fry for 15 minutes at 180 degrees Celsius.

Air Fried Potato Crisps

Preparation time: 45 minutes
Cooking time: 8 minutes
Serves: 2 people

Ingredients:

- 3 large baking potatoes
- 1 tablespoon of olive oil

- 1 teaspoon of sea salt
- 1/2 teaspoon of roast chicken seasoning (optional)
- 1/2 teaspoon of garlic powder (optional)
- 1/2 teaspoon of beef seasoning (optional)

Method:

1. Thinly slice your potatoes and place into a large bowl of water.
2. Drain the water from your sliced potatoes and pat them dry.
3. Leave to air dry for 10 minutes.
4. Season your potatoes with the olive oil and the sea salt.
5. Air fry for 8 minutes at 180 degrees Celsius or until crispy.
6. Toss in either beef, chicken or garlic powder depending on which flavour crisps you would like. Different dried herbs can also be fun flavour combinations! You can split the crisps into groups to make a few different flavours from one batch.

Breaded Babybel Cheese Bites

Preparation time: 10 minutes
Cooking time: 10 minutes
Serves: 10 breaded cheeses
Ingredients:

- 2 large eggs
- 200 g of unwrapped Babybel cheese
- 25g ketchup
- 1 tablespoon sweet chilli sauce
- 40 g white flour
- 400g breadcrumbs
- 25g barbecue sauce

Method:

1. Whisk the egg and place in one bowl with the flour in another and the breadcrumbs in a third bowl.
2. Dip the cheeses into the flour then eggs then the breadcrumbs.
3. Place in the air fryer tray.
4. Air fry at 170 degrees Celsius for 5-10 minutes until the outside is golden brown.
5. Mix the barbecue sauce, ketchup and sweet chilli sauce together and serve as a dip.

Mozzarella Chips

Preparation time: 20 minutes
Cooking time: 5 minutes
Serves: 8 pieces
Ingredients:

- 2 tablespoons of white flour
- 2 large eggs
- 550 g mozzarella in a block
- 3 teaspoons of garlic powder
- 150g breadcrumbs

Method:

1. Mix flour and garlic powder in one bowl.
2. In another bowl whisk the eggs.
3. Place breadcrumbs in a third bowl.
4. Slice mozzarella into 2 cm thick strips.
5. Dip the mozzarella into the flour, then the egg and finally the breadcrumbs.
6. Spray air fryer tray and mozzarella sticks with non stick cooking spray.
7. Air fry for 4 to 5 minutes in batches at 180 degrees Celsius.

Triple Cheese Balls

Preparation time: 10 minutes
Cooking time: 15 minutes
Serves: 14 balls
Ingredients:

- 80 g grated cheddar
- 70g grated parmesan
- 2 teaspoons of cajun seasoning
- Non stick cooking spray
- 85 g cottage cheese
- 75 g white flour
- 2 eggs, lightly beaten

Method:

1. Mix the cheeses, flour, seasoning and eggs in a large bowl.
2. Roll out balls of about 1 tablespoon of mixture.
3. Spray balls with non stick cooking spray.
4. Place in air fryer tray and fry at 180 degree Celsius for 10-12 minutes.

Crackling Crisps

Preparation time: 5 minutes
Cooking time: 30 minutes
Serves: 6 people
Ingredients:

- 750g pork rind
- 1/2 teaspoon of sea salt flakes
- 2 teaspoons of bacon seasoning
- 1/4 teaspoon of black pepper

Method:

1. Cut the rind crossways into small strips.
2. Allow rind to dry out overnight.
3. Spray air fryer tray with non stick cooking spray.
4. Place rind in tray and spray with cooking spray then sprinkle with bacon seasoning.
5. Air fry at 200 degrees Celsius for 10-15 minutes until bubbling.
6. Toss the crackling in the sea salt flakes and the black pepper.

Halloumi Popcorn

Preparation time: 20 minutes
Cooking time: 10 minutes
Serves: 4 people

Ingredients:

- 2 teaspoons of smoked paprika
- 1 teaspoon of mustard powder
- 1 teaspoon of onion powder
- 225g halloumi, cubed
- 60g breadcrumbs
- 1 teaspoon of brown sugar
- 1 teaspoon of cornflour
- 1/2 teaspoon of garlic powder
- 2 eggs

Method:

1. Preheat your air fryer to 180 degrees Celsius.
2. Mix together the paprika, sugar, mustard powder, cornflour, onion powder and garlic powder in a dish.
3. Add the halloumi and coat each piece gently.
4. Beat the eggs and dip each piece of halloumi into the egg then the breadcrumbs.
5. Place the halloumi into the air fryer and fry for 8 to 10 minutes or until golden brown.

Mini Oreo Cheesecakes

Preparation time: 45 minutes
Cooking time: 30 minutes
Serves: 10 mini cheesecakes

Ingredients:

- 10 Oreos
- 1 beaten egg
- Whipped cream (to serve)
- 250 g cream cheese
- 64 g chopped Mars bars

Method:

1. Line air fryer tray with muffin cases.
2. Split the Oreo cookies and place one half cream side up in each muffin case.
3. Beat the cream cheese and add the egg.
4. Melt all the Mars bars and add to the cream cheese.
5. Spoon 2 tablespoons of the mixture onto each Oreo cookie in the muffin cases.
6. Top with the other half of the Oreo cookies.
7. Air fry in batches for 8-10 minutes at 160 degrees Celsius.
8. Serve topped with a little whipped cream.

Easy Garlic-Rosemary Brussels Sprouts

Preparation time: 30 minutes
Cooking time: 15-20 minutes
Serves: 4 people

Ingredients:

- 450g Brussels Sprouts
- 3 Minced Cloves of Garlic
- 1/4 Teaspoon of Black Pepper
- 30 g of Breadcrumbs

- 3 Tablespoons of Olive Oil
- 1/2 Teaspoon of Salt
- 1 Teaspoon of Minced Rosemary

Method:

1. Start by preparing your air fryer on the roast setting.
2. Next add your olive oil, minced garlic, salt and pepper into a microwave-safe bowl and mix thoroughly. Microwave on the high setting for thirty-seconds.
3. Afterwards, grab your Brussels sprouts and toss them in half of the microwaved mixture. Then you can place your sprouts onto the air fryer tray.
4. Roast your sprouts for four to five minutes then take them out to stir and continue roasting for another seven or eight minutes. Remember to take them out halfway to turn them again.
5. Next, combine the rosemary and your breadcrumbs with the other half of your microwaved mixture. Add the mixture over your sprouts and cook for around five minutes.
6. These sprouts taste best-served piping hot alongside a roast dinner!

Turkey and Brie Parcels with Cranberry Sauce

Preparation time: 15 minutes
Cooking time: 10 minutes
Serves: 4 people

Ingredients:

- 4 Turkey Breasts chopped
- 4 Tablespoons of Brie
- 1 egg, lightly beaten

- 4 Tablespoons of Cranberry sauce
- 4 sheets of frozen shortcrust pastry

Method:

1. Lightly fry your turkey breast in a frying pan.
2. Unroll your pastry sheets and cut into 1 inch squares.
3. Place a small amount of the cooked turkey, brie and cranberry sauce in the middle of each square.

4. Close the squares by sandwiching the filling between another square of pastry.

5. Crimp edges closed with a fork.

6. Brush the tops with the beaten egg and pierce gently with a fork.

7. Fry in your air fryer for 10 minutes or until golden brown on 190 degrees Celsius.

Pork Belly with a Christmas Glaze

Preparation time: 10 minutes
Cooking time: 55 minutes
Serves: 4 people

Ingredients:

- 1kg pork belly
- 4 small pink lady apples
- 60 ml apple cider vinegar
- 2 teaspoons of mustard
- 40g chilled, chopped butter
- 1 teaspoon of salt
- 125ml maple syrup
- 55g caster sugar
- 1/2 teaspoons of mixed spice

Method:

1. Preheat air fryer to 200 degrees Celsius.

2. Rub salt into the pork belly.

3. Spray air fryer basket with non stick cooking spray.

4. Place pork in the basket and spray with cooking spray.

5. Air fry the pork for 25 minutes.

6. Reduce the temperature to 160 degrees Celsius.

7. Slice the apples and add to the basket. Air fry for a further 30 minutes.

8. Prepare the glaze by mixing maple syrup, vinegar, sugar, mustard and the spice in a small saucepan. Cover and boil.

9. Reduce heat and simmer for 5 minutes then add the butter.

10. Slice and serve your pork and cover with the festive glaze.

Simple Corn Casserole

Preparation time: 10 minutes
Cooking time: 55 minutes
Serves: 10 people

Ingredients:

- 1 large tin of sweetcorn
- 100g melted butter
- 1/4 teaspoon of salt
- 1/4 teaspoon of garlic powder
- 200 g sour cream
- 1 packet of bread mix
- 1/4 teaspoon of pepper
- 1/4 teaspoon of oregano

Method:

1. Add all your ingredients except the seasonings to a bowl and mix well.
2. Gently fold in the seasonings allowing them to mix through the mixture well.
3. Spray air fryer tray with non stick cooking spray.
4. Spoon mixture into the tray.
5. Air fry for 50-55 minutes at 190 degrees Celsius.

Vegetarian Christmas Log

Preparation time: 20 minutes
Cooking time: 20 minutes
Serves: 6 people

Ingredients:

- 1 tablespoon of olive oil
- 3 crushed garlic gloves
- 500 g frozen spinach previously thawed
- 180g halloumi grated
- 3 eggs, one beaten

- 1 brown onion, finely chopped
- 2 teaspoons fresh thyme leaves
- 300g crumbled ricotta
- 1 tablespoon grated lemon rind
- 2 1/2 sheets frozen puff pastry, thawed

Method:

1. Heat the oil in a frying pan.
2. Add the onion, garlic and thyme and cook for 5 minutes.
3. Add the spinach, ricotta, halloumi and lemon to the onion mixture. Then add the two eggs.
4. Mix well and season to taste.
5. Place the 2 pastry sheets onto a floured surface and put the spinach mixture in the centre of each sheet. Roll up the sheets.
6. Brush with the beaten egg and add festive shapes with the leftover pastry.
7. Heat in the air fryer at 180 degrees Celsius for 15 minutes or until the filling is heated through.

Mulled Wine

Preparation time: 10 minutes
Cooking time: 6 minutes
Serves: 12 people

Ingredients:

- L 1.5 red wine
- 150g honey
- 1 apple (thinly sliced)
- 1 teaspoon of black peppercorns

- 100ml spiced rum
- juice and peel of 2 mandarins
- peel of 2 lemons
- 1 vanilla pod

- 2 star anise
- 2" piece of fresh ginger
- 1/2 teaspoon of allspice
- 1 cinnamon stick
- 1/4 teaspoon of nutmeg
- 6 cloves

Method:

1. Add all your ingredients to your air fryer basket.
2. Cook on 180 degrees Celsius for 5 minutes.
3. Set your air fryer to the keep warm setting and enjoy all evening.

Brie and Cranberry stuffed Chicken

Preparation time: 15 minutes
Cooking time: 10 minutes
Serves: 4 people

Ingredients:

- 4 Chicken Breasts
- 4 Tablespoons of Brie
- 1/4 teaspoon of salt
- 4 Tablespoons of Cranberry sauce
- 1 1/2 Tablespoons of olive oil
- 1/4 teaspoon of pepper

Method:

1. Each chicken breast should have a pocket that is as broad as feasible without cutting through, so insert a knife into the thickest section of each breast and slide it back and forth.
2. Using a spoon, distribute the brie and cranberry sauce among the pockets. Rub in the remaining 1/2 tbsp of oil and season with salt and pepper.
3. Air fry for ten minutes at 190 degrees Celsius.

Creamed Brussels Sprouts

Preparation time: 30 minutes
Cooking time: 35 minutes
Serves: 6 people

Ingredients:

- 1 tablespoon olive oil
- 3 minced garlic cloves
- 1/2 teaspoon crushed red pepper flakes
- 1/4 teaspoon of black pepper
- 100g mayonnaise
- 100 g cheddar cheese, grated
- 1/2 yellow onion, chopped
- 1kg brussels sprouts
- 1/4 teaspoon salt
- 200 g greek yoghurt
- 2 lightly beaten eggs
- 100g parmesan, grated

Method:

1. In a large frying pan combine the onion and garlic and cook until softened.

2. Next add the Brussels sprouts and red pepper flakes. Cook for 7 minutes.
3. Season with salt and pepper then let cool.
4. Mix the yoghurt, mayonnaise, eggs and cheese.
5. Add the vegetables to the yoghurt mixture.
6. Bake at 190 degrees Celsius in your air fryer for 30-35 minutes.

Simple Pigs in Blankets

Preparation time: 5 minutes
Cooking time: 12 minutes
Serves: 4 people

Ingredients:

- 8 rashers of streaky bacon
- 2 tablespoons of honey
- 1 tablespoon of butter
- 8 pork chipolata sausages
- 1 tablespoon of caster sugar

Method:

1. Each shipload must be wrapped in a single rasher of bacon before being placed in the air fryer basket in a single layer.
2. Cook the bacon and chipolatas for 10 to 12 minutes at 180°C, or until they are fully cooked. Keep an eye on the sausages and cook for a few minutes longer if you like your bacon extra-crisp.
3. While the pigs in blankets are air frying, combine the butter, sugar and honey in a saucepan and melt until the sugar dissolves. For the final 2 minutes of cooking, brush the pigs in blankets with the glaze.

Air Fried Parsnips with Maple and Hazelnuts

Preparation time: 10 minutes
Cooking time: 1 hour
Serves: 4 people

Ingredients:

- 1 tablespoon of olive oil
- 50g maple syrup
- 1/2 teaspoon of sea salt flakes
- 1/4 teaspoon of parsley
- 1/4 teaspoon of thyme
- 750g parsnips, peeled, trimmed and quartered.
- 50g chopped hazelnuts
- 1/4 teaspoon of black pepper
- 1/4 teaspoon of rosemary

Methods:

1. Preheat your air fryer to 200 degrees Celsius.
2. Put the parsnips in the air fryer tray and toss in oil.

3. Air fry for 50 minutes.

4. Drizzle with the maple syrup and toss in the hazelnuts and seasonings.

5. Air fry for a further 10 minutes or until the parsnips are golden brown.

Air Fryer Brie

Preparation time: 5 minutes

Cooking time: 10 minutes

Serves: 4 people

Ingredients:

- 125ml honey
- 1 fresh rosemary sprig with the leaves picked
- 1 crusty baguette
- 125g dried figs, quartered
- 300g brie
- 2 tablespoons of olive oil

Method:

1. Simmer the honey, figs and rosemary in a saucepan for 3 minutes then set aside to cool.

2. Meanwhile, cute the baguette into small cubes and drizzle with olive oil.

3. Place the brie in a ramekin then into the air fryer basket alongside the bread pieces.

4. Air fry at 180 degrees Celsius for 6 minutes.

5. Drizzle the honey mixture over the brie and serve.

Air Fryer Turkey Breast

Preparation time: 5 minutes

Cooking time: 1 hour

Serves: 6 people

Ingredients:

- 2 kg boneless turkey breast
- 1/2 teaspoon of salt
- 1/2 teaspoon of rosemary
- 1/4 teaspoon of black pepper
- 2 tablespoons of melted butter
- 1/2 teaspoon of thyme
- 1/2 teaspoon of sage

Method:

1. Pat your turkey down using a paper towel.

2. Combine your seasonings and melted butter.

3. Brush your flavoured butter all over the turkey.

4. Place your turkey in the air fryer tray.

5. Fry at 180 degrees Celsius for 1 hour, turning halfway through.

Celebration Chocolate Bites

Preparation time: 15 minutes
Cooking time: 10 minutes
Serves: 24 bites

Ingredients:

- 4 sheets of frozen shortcrust pastry
- 24 celebration chocolates
- 50g icing sugar (optional)
- 1 egg, lightly beaten
- 3 tablespoons of icing sugar (optional)
- 2 teaspoon water (optional)

Method:

1. Unroll your pastry and wrap each celebration chocolate in the pastry.
2. Line the parcels up in your air fryer tray.
3. Brush the tops with the egg.
4. Fry for 10 minutes or until the tops are golden brown at 190 degrees Celsius.
5. Dust with icing sugar and serve or mix the icing sugar and water to create a tasty glaze.
6. Drizzle the glaze in a zig zag over the chocolate bites or serve in a small dish as a sweet dip.

Easy Peppermint Brownies

Preparation time: 10 minutes
Cooking time: 15 minutes
Serves: 16 brownies

Ingredients:

- 120 ml whole milk
- 200 g white flour
- 150g margarine
- 1 large egg
- 1/4 teaspoon peppermint essence
- 50 g crushed peppermints or candy canes
- 1 banana
- 100g coco powder
- 50g sugar
- 1 teaspoon baking powder

Method:

1. Preheat your air fryer to 200 degrees Celsius.
2. Melt your margarine.
3. Combine the sugar, whisked egg and margarine.
4. Next, add the coco, flour, baking powder, peppermint essence and mashed banana. Then stir in the milk.
5. Top with crushed peppermints.
6. Cook for between 10 and 15 minutes in your air fryer. It is better to take them out a little too soon so the brownies remain fudgey.

Spiced Nuts

Preparation time: 10 minutes
Cooking time: 20 minutes
Serves: 6 people

Ingredients:

- 1 1/2 tablespoons of honey
- 1 crushed clove of garlic
- 1 tablespoon of smoked paprika
- 200g almond kernels
- 200g macadamia nuts
- 2 tablespoons of olive oil
- 1/4 teaspoon chilli powder
- 1 teaspoon of salt
- 200g cashew nuts
- 200g brazil nuts

Method:

1. Preheat your air fryer to 190 degrees Celsius and spray tray with a non stick cooking spray.
2. Combine the honey, olive oil, garlic, chilli, paprika and salt in a frying pan on low heat. Keep on the heat and stir until the honey has melted.
3. Mix the honey mixture with the nuts.
4. Spread the coated nuts across the air fryer tray and fry in batches for 15 minutes.

Pasta Chips

Preparation time: 4 minutes
Cooking time: 35 minutes
Serves: 4-6 people

Ingredients:

- 200g pasta
- 2 teaspoons of smoked paprika
- 1 teaspoon of onion powder
- 2 teaspoons chives
- 2 tablespoons olive oil
- 1 teaspoons of ground cumin
- 25g sour cream
- 25g cream cheese

Method:

1. Cook your pasta as you normally would or follow the instructions on the packaging.
2. Add the olive oil and seasoning then mix thoroughly.
3. Set your air fryer to 180 degrees Celsius and cook for 20 minutes, shaking every 5 minutes.
4. Combine your cream cheese and sour cream.
5. Mix in the chives.
6. Serve as a dip alongside your pasta chips!

Tofu Nuggets

Preparation time: 15 minutes
Cooking time: 15 minutes
Serves: 24 nuggets

Ingredients:

- 1 block of extra firm tofu
- 1 1/2 teaspoon of smoked paprika
- 125 ml milk
- 1 1/2 teaspoon of garlic powder

- 4 tablespoons white flour
- 1 teaspoon mustard
- 75 g breadcrumbs
- 1 tablespoon of bouillon powder

Method:

1. Wrap your tofu block in clingfilm and press under a heavy object for 30 minutes.
2. Cut the tofu into cubes.
3. Toss with the tablespoon of flour and paprika.
4. Combine the remaining flour, mustard and milk.
5. Mix the other ingredients together and tip onto a tray.
6. Preheat air fryer to 190 degrees Celsius.
7. Coat the tofu in the milk, then the flour and finally the breadcrumbs.
8. Place in the air fryer tray and fry for 15 minutes.

Air-Fried Healthier Doughnuts

Preparation time: 30 minutes (Plus overnight proving time)
Cooking time: 25 minutes
Serves: Around 6 doughnuts

Ingredients:

- 125ml milk
- 1 sachet of dried yeast
- 1 teaspoon of vanilla extract
- 1 large egg
- 50g unsalted butter,
- 60g caster sugar
- 275 g of plain flour, plus extra for dusting
- A little flavourless oil for proving

For the Glaze and Decorations:

- 125g icing sugar
- 3 tablespoons of milk
- Sprinkles

Method:

1. Start off by melting the butter. Next, in a large bowl mix the milk (room temperature), melted butter, yeast, 1 teaspoon of sugar, and vanilla extract. The yeast needs 8 to 10 minutes to activate.

2. The remaining sugar, flour and 1/2 teaspoon salt should all be combined in a separate bowl. The milk mixture should be combined with the beaten egg before the dry ingredients are added. The dough should be smooth and elastic after 5-8 minutes of medium-speed kneading with a dough hook. The dough can also be smoothed out by hand kneading for 10 to 12 minutes. You should be left with quite a sticky dough!

3. Transfer to a bowl that has been lightly oiled, cover with a fresh tea towel and let the dough rise for one and a half hours, or until it has doubled in size. Lay the dough out and roll it out to a thickness of about 1.5 cm on a lightly dusted surface. Use a doughnut cutter or two cutters to make your doughnuts (1 x 7.5 cm and 1 x 2.5 cm for the middle). If desired, place the doughnut centres with the doughnuts on a lined baking sheet. Then, cover it with a fresh tea towel. Allow it to rise in the refrigerator overnight or for 40 minutes. If left overnight the doughnuts will be a little more doughnut-shaped and easier to work with.

4. When ready to cook, insert a few doughnuts (with their centres, if saving them) in the air fryer basket and cook, as directed by the manufacturer, at 180C for 5–6 minutes, or until golden. Remove from the basket and let the doughnuts to cool on a wire rack while you prepare the remaining doughnuts (bearing in mind that certain air fryers generate more intense heat, so keep checking to make sure the doughnuts don't burn). If you're concerned that the doughnuts will adhere to the basket and that indentations from the basket will form on the doughnuts, you can insert a sheet of baking paper at the bottom of the basket.

5. Sift the icing sugar into a bowl and whisk in the milk as the last batch of doughnuts bake. Dip the top of each doughnut in the glaze once they have cooled. The glaze should be left to set on a wire rack. If desired, add sprinkles while the glaze is still wet!

Yummy Air Fryer Muffins

Preparation time: 10 minutes
Cooking time: 15 minutes
Serves: 6 people

Ingredients:

- 60 ml vegetable oil
- 1 egg
- 100g caster sugar
- 1/4 teaspoon of bicarbonate of soda
- 75 g natural yoghurt
- 2 tablespoons of whole milk
- 150 g self-raising flour
- 75 g of your desired topping

Method:

1. 2 minutes at 160C will warm up the air fryer. In a large bowl, combine the oil, yoghurt, egg, and milk.
2. Next, add the sugar, flour, and bicarbonate of soda and stir to thoroughly blend.
3. Now fold in the topping of your choice. Pour the mixture into silicone liners or a muffin tray for air fryers. Although you might need to bake the muffins in batches, you should be able to make 6 to 8 of them.
4. Place the cases or tin in the air fryer basket and cook for 12 to 15 minutes. You can check to see if the muffins are ready by poking a skewer in the middle of one and if it comes out clean then it is ready!

Quick, Simple Hand Pies

Preparation time:
Cooking time:
Serves:

Ingredients:

- 2 apples
- 2 generous tablespoons of light brown sugar
- 1 tablespoon of caster sugar plus extra for sprinkling
- 1/2 teaspoon of ground cinnamon
- 1/8 teaspoon of salt
- 1 tablespoon of apple juice
- 1 large egg yolk mixed with water
- 1 package of pre-made puff pastry
- 150g raspberries

Method:

1. Apples, raspberries, sugar, cinnamon, salt, and apple juice or cider should all be combined in a medium pot. Over medium heat, bring to a simmer; then; cover and lower heat. Cook for about 15 minutes, stirring periodically until apples start to soften but still keep their structure.

2. Cook for 1-2 minutes, stirring occasionally, on medium heat, until thickened. Take off of the heat and allow it to cool to room temperature.

3. Unroll pie crusts while the filling cools. Using a cookie cutter, cut the dough into 4-inch circles, rerolling the scraps as necessary. There should be 12 circles.

4. Each circle should have a tablespoon of filling in the centre. After lightly moistening the dough's edges, fold it over the filling and press to seal. Avoid overfilling.

5. To crimp the sealed edges, use a fork. Use a paring knife's tip to make two tiny slits on the top of each pie after lightly brushing the pies with egg wash. Sugar should be added to the tops.

6. Set your air fryer's temperature to 160 degrees Celsius. Six pies at a time, add them in a single layer and bake for 15 minutes, or until the tops are brown.

Easy Cinnamon Pear Cake

Preparation time: 15 minutes
Cooking time: 25-30 minutes
Serves: 8 slices

Ingredients:

- 240 g all-purpose flour
- 1 teaspoon of baking powder
- 1 large or 2 medium eggs

- 200g caster sugar
- 170 g of cold margarine
- 120 ml whole milk

For the Topping:

- 4 tablespoons of caster sugar
- 2 tablespoons of cinnamon
- 3 large ripe pears or 4 to 5 smaller ripe pears

Method:

1. Preheat your air fryer to 200 degrees Celsius and grease the cake pan attachment.

2. Combine the flour, sugar, baking powder and all of the margarine in a large mixing bowl. I suggest mixing with a fork. Make sure your margarine is cold during this process and mix until the ingredients reassemble a fine breadcrumb mixture.

3. Whisk the egg(s) thoroughly and add to the mixture along with the milk. Stir until creamy but not firm.

4. Add the rest of the sugar and flour and stir.

5. Place the completed mixture into your greased cake pan.

6. Top and tail your pears, and then cut into quarters. Afterwards, slice the pears thinly and arrange them in a fan shape across the cake.

7. Combine your cinnamon and sugar, then sprinkle over the top of your pears.

8. Bake for 30 minutes in your air fryer or until a knife comes out of the cake cleanly.

Easy Air Fryer Brownies

Preparation time: 10 minutes
Cooking time: 15 minutes
Serves: 16 brownies

Ingredients:

- 120 ml whole milk
- 200 g white flour
- 150g margarine
- 1 large egg
- 1 teaspoon baking powder
- 1 banana
- 100g coco powder
- 50g sugar
- 1 tablespoon of honey

Method:

1. Preheat your air fryer to 200 degrees Celsius.
2. Melt your margarine.
3. Combine the sugar, whisked egg and margarine.
4. Next, add the coco, flour, baking powder, honey and mashed banana. Then stir in the milk
5. Cook for between 10 and 15 minutes in your air fryer. It is better to take them out a little too soon so the brownies remain fudgey.

Super Easy Apple Pie

Preparation time: 10 minutes
Cooking time: 15 minutes
Serves: 8 slices

Ingredients:

- Two large apples
- 1 teaspoon of cinnamon
- 50 g sugar (plus extra for sprinkling)
- 2 packages of pre made shortcrust pastry
- cinnamon sticks and apple slices to serve with as a garnish

Method:

1. Chop the apples into small chunks and cook on the stove with the sugar until the apples are softened and the juices have made a syrupy liquid.
2. Line the air fryer cake pan with 1 package of pre made pastry.
3. Add the apple mixture.

4. Cut the second package of pastry into strips and arrange in a lattice over the apples.

5. Crimp the edges with a fork.

6. Bake in your air fryer for 15 minutes at 180 degrees Celsius, sprinkling the remaining sugar on the top for the final five minutes.

Giant Cookie

Preparation time: 10 minutes
Cooking time 10 minutes
Serves: 8 slices of cookie

Ingredients:

- 150g softened butter
- 80g caster sugar
- 1 large egg
- 1/2 teaspoon of bicarbonate soda
- 200g chocolate chips
- 80 g light brown muscovado sugar
- 2 teaspoons of vanilla extract
- 225 g white flour
- 1/4 teaspoon of salt

Method:

1. Preheat your air fryer to 190 degrees Celsius.

2. Add the butter and both kinds of sugar to a bowl and mix until a creamy consistency.

3. Add the vanilla extract and the whisked egg.

4. Slowly mix in the flour, bicarbonate soda and salt. Stir well.

5. Add your chocolate chips.

6. Spread the mixture out over the air fryer cake pan attachment.

7. Bake for 8-10 minutes until the cookie has a slightly browned edge.

Churros

Preparation time: 1 hour
Cooking time: 10 minutes
Serves: 4 people

Ingredients:

- 200 ml water
- 2 tablespoons of sugar
- 200 g white flour
- 1 teaspoon of vanilla extract
- 100g sugar
- 66g unsalted butter
- 1/4 teaspoon of salt
- 2 large eggs
- oil based cooking spray
- 3/4 teaspoon of ground cinnamon

Method:

1. Spray air fryer tray with cooking spray.

2. Heat the water, butter, sugar and salt in a medium saucepan and bring to a boil.

3. Reduce heat and add the flour and keep stirring until it forms a dough.

4. Remove from the heat and place dough in a large bowl.

5. Allow dough to cool.

6. Add the eggs and vanilla extract and mix thoroughly.

7. Put mixture into a large piping bag.

8. Pipe the churros directly into air fryer tray. Aim for 4 inch churros.

9. Place the tray into the fridge and let rest for one hour.

10. Take out the fridge and spray churros with cooking spray.

11. Place in air fryer and fry for 10-12 minutes at 190 degrees Celsius.

12. Combine the rest of the sugar and cinnamon and roll the churros in the mixture.

Air Fried Oreos

Preparation time: 5 minutes
Cooking time: 5 minutes
Serves: 4 people
Ingredients:

- 8 Oreo cookies
- 3 tablespoons of icing sugar (optional)
- 1 teaspoon water (optional)
- 1 can of croissant dough
- 10g icing sugar (optional)

Method:

1. Preheat the air fryer to 150 degrees Celsius.

2. Cover each Oreo in a piece of the croissant dough.

3. Place each Oreo into the air fryer basket.

4. Fry in the air fryer for 5-6 minutes, turning halfway through.

5. Sprinkle the fried Oreos with the icing sugar.(optional)

6. Or combine the 10g icing sugar with water and make a tasty icing glaze to drizzle your Oreos with. You can also serve with melted chocolate.

Air Fried Shortbread

Preparation time:10 minutes
Cooking time: 8 minutes
Serves: 4 people
Ingredients:

- 6 tablespoons of butter
- 150 g white flour
- 20g butter, softened
- 50g icing sugar
- 50g icing sugar extra

Method:

1. Combine the butter and sugar until a creamy mixture is formed.

2. Slowly add the 150 g of white flour until it becomes a dough.

3. Roll the dough into a log and wrap in cling film. Place in the fridge for 30 minutes.

4. Slice the dough into 1/2 inch thick discs and place in the greased air fryer tray.

5. Bake for 8-10 minutes at 180 degrees Celsius.

6. Mix the butter and other icing sugar thoroughly to form a delicious buttercream icing.

Banana Porridge Cookies

Preparation time: 5 minutes
Cooking time: 10 minutes
Serves: 4 cookies

Ingredients:

- 1 large banana
- 2 tablespoons of raisins
- 1/4 teaspoon of ginger
- 100g oats
- 1/4 teaspoon of cinnamon
- Zest of 1 orange

Method:

1. Peel and mash your banana.

2. Combine the oats, mashed banana, cinnamon, ginger, orange zest and raisins.

3. Shape into small cookies.

4. Place into air fryer basket.

5. Cook for 8-10 minutes at 150 degrees Celsius.

Peanut Butter Biscuits

Preparation time: 35 minutes
Cooking time: 15 minutes
Serves: 10 biscuits

Ingredients:

- 200 g soft light brown sugar
- 225g crunchy peanut butter, plus an extra 5 tablespoons that has been melted
- 100g melted chocolate
- 1 large egg

Method:

1. Mix the sugar and egg until smooth then add the peanut butter and mix until combined.

2. Cover with clingfilm and let chill for 30 minutes.

3. Preheat air fryer at 180 degrees Celsius.

4. Roll the dough into 10 small balls and place in air fryer tray. You may need to cook in small batches.

5. Bake for 12-15 minutes or until the edges are golden brown.

6. Dip your finished biscuits in melted chocolate and drizzle with melted peanut butter.

Printed in Great Britain
by Amazon

20235262R00045